For Robin Wilson —
    with great admiration &
best wishes for your valued
leadership of TWA!
    Happy Landings always!
                Walt Gunn

P.S. This book written to capture
some of the 25 million fearful
flyers for TWA!!

THE JOY OF FLYING: Overcoming the FEAR
Copyright (C) 1987 by Wings Publications

Wings Publications
P.O. Box 161
Mission, Kansas 66201
U.S.A.

Library of Congress Cataloging-in-Publication Data

Gunn, Walter Howard.
The Joy of Flying: Overcoming the Fear.
Library of Congress Catalog Card No. 87-50734
ISBN 0-9618817-0-4
Second Printing 1989
Original cover by Nancy Sams
Photo credit to Al Clegg, PSA

Printed by Intercollegiate Press Mission, Kansas, USA

Table Of Contents

Chapter 1 — The Fear of Flying (Apologies to Erica Jong)

Aerophobia is universal and non-discriminating. Fear of flying ranks second only to the fear of public speaking. Impressive air safety records fail to convince those stricken with an irrational fear of flight. Although most of these fears are without basis in fact, they can cause deep anxiety and physical discomfort — unnecessarily imprisoning the aerophobic.

Chapter 2 — "This is Your Captain Speaking"

There's more to alleviating the fear of flying than encouragement from the Captain, although his comments can be soothing. Even movie tough guys, champion athletes, and world-famous persons can develop "anticipatory" anxiety attacks, but overt panic is indeed rare! Avoiding flight only prolongs the fear. Flight crews, when called upon, can be more effective than "shrinks" in allaying anxiety in flight.

Chapter 3 — "This is Your Psychologist Speaking"

Does flying have deep symbolic meanings with underlying sexual connotations? Is the fear of flying involved with the repression of inner conflicts? Psychoanalysts may think so, but "couch" therapy is unnecessary. Fears and phobias related to flying are described. Important social factors are considered. The role of anxiety is highlighted. Treatment can be "painless" — with surprising benefits in coping with other problems of living.

Chapter 4 — When Fear Interferes, The Body Defends

What happens to your body, physically, when fear strikes? Most fears are learned responses which can be controlled, even unlearned, with guided effort. When rational, stress, anxiety, and even fear can be used positively. Irrationally, the body pays for the emotional drain.

Chapter 5 — Profiles of Aerophobia

Many personality factors contribute to aerophobia. Faulty attitudes and beliefs underlie the "chronic doubting" of those suffering phobic disorders. Aerophobia comprises four personality patterns consisting of: 1) generalized anxiety, 2) problems of control (of self, or others), 3) separation anxiety, and 4) claustrophobia. Could any of these problems remind you of someone — If not yourself — a friend perchance?

Chapter 6 — Case Studies: Successes and Failures

Real life accounts of a cross-section of clients in a fear of flying program. Emotional problems vary, but anguish is constant. Surprises abound when underlying factors are revealed. When dealt with, positive gains result! When denied or avoided, fear persists. Identifying with another's flying fears provides valuable insight and viable options for change — to **succeed** or **fail.** The choice is theirs!

Chapter 7 — Gaining Control over Fear

Although gaining control over your fear is not a simple process, there are many practical and learnable methods for managing anxiety and fear. Learning to relax pays handsomely. Stress management benefits many. Medication is helpful with prudent use. Rational control of feelings and thoughts overcomes the irrational pangs of aerophobia. Adaptive change results. Fear diminishes. Flying becomes bearable.

Chapter 8 — Everything You Wanted to Know About Flying (But were afraid to ask)

Undue concerns dissolve when flight is demystified. Myriad ''whatifs'' are answered. Facts are given about weather, navigation, traffic control, terrorism, and accidents, along with titillating trivia about the Jumbo 747. Gaining confidence countermands doubt!

Chapter 9 — You ARE in Good Hands

Today's airline crews, both flight and ground, are well-trained, thoughtful and caring persons who take their responsibilities seriously. Meet your airline crews and learn of their training — EXERCISE IN EXCELLENCE — to be assured that in their hands, you will have a safe and comfortable flight. The goal for all: HAPPY LANDINGS ALWAYS.

ACKNOWLEDGEMENTS

Many friends and colleagues (in aviation and academia) deserve recognition for their encouragement and contribution in the completion of this book.

Aviation has been a major life-long vocational interest. Psychology has held a secondary role until my retirement from airline flying.

While flying with TWA, the following pilots — Captains all - made lasting impressions (most of them unknowingly), which have served as a challenge to further enhance aviation. Love of flying is our common bond. My heartfelt appreciation is due them — all valued friends:

Harold Aikin

Fred Austin

Bob Buck

Ed Frankum

Jack Frye (Pres.)

Floyd Hall

Marv Horstman

Benny Howard

Harold Neumann

Vern Laursen

Orv Olson

Carter Burgess,
(Hon. Capt.)

Now, in the role of teacher, I am able to continue serving aviation. Many academic friendships evolved "enroute" to my becoming a psychologist. To mention but a few:

Drs. Bill Arndt and Bernie Kleinman made graduate studies pleasurable at the University of Missouri-Kansas City. Dr. Marshall Saper, radio psychologist and friend since graduate school, encouraged writing this book.

Dr. Norris Haring enrichened post-graduate endeavors while I was a psychologist under his mentorship at the Kansas University Children's Rehabilitation Unit.

More recently, associates in the Department of Psychiatry at the Kansas University Medical Center have helped to fill a void since airline retirement, by peaking my interest in programs of alcohol research, stress management, and aerophobia. They are:

Don Goodwin, M.D., Chairman and author, whom I envy in his professional acumen and journalistic skills. Others on his staff whose

acquaintances I have enjoyed as an associate are Ron Martin, M.D., Paul Laybourne, M.D., Betty Penick, Ph.D., Manuel Pardo, M.D., Fowler Jones, Ed.D., Tom Kent, M.D., Gene Harpster, M.D. and flight surgeon, and for a much longer period of rewarding friendship, Bill McKnelly, M.D.

Medical students Jim Otto, Brad Marples, Mike Jones, and Bill Frost — now M.D.'s all — were youthfully refreshing in research project consultations professionally and socially.

The Aviation Department at Central Missouri State University under Dr. Jack Horine's direction has afforded me an opportunity to stay abreast of aviation academically. CMSU can take pride in its aviation program and I heartily endorse it to those aspiring for a career in aviation technology and flying. Much credit is due Fred Schieszer, Roger Mason, Bob Mock, Tom Hemphill, and Dean Rawleigh Gaines.

Captain John Testrake, TWA, and Captain Charley Plumb, USNR, both of whom shun the "hero" label for their feats of courage and concern for others during life-threatening times, deserve recognition as "model pilots-in-command!" Their humble attitude offers encouragement for others being able to call forth those inner strengths that help banish fear.

The lifelong friendship of Dr. Othello Dale Smith, M.D. has provided valued counsel in every undertaking. Dale had his first airplane ride in my Porterfield trainer in 1942 before becoming a B-17 pilot in the Eighth Air Force, and later, a physician and worldly scholar.

My brother George, Air Force fighter test pilot (and Sigma Tau Gamma fraternity brother as well), played a key role in my formative years and aviation career. George is a true survivor having managed fear during a near-tragedy in his test-flying days. His parachute was well-packed! His son, Terry Gunn follows as a TWA pilot today.

Appreciation of manuscript assistance is due Carl Foster, CMSU. Lisa Knight, UMKC and Dr. Mike Morra, aviation psychologist. Dr. Doug Moore, educator, psycholinguist and communications critic offered major editing suggestions to enhance my writing — through a greater use of the active voice — which was first attempted eons ago by Helen Jo Crissman, my Paseo High School journalism teacher.

Uppermost, heartfelt gratitude is due my immediate family for indulging the "stress of creativity" during the gestation period of this book.

Dedicated to
Lu, Nance, Tim, and Rick

ABOUT THE AUTHOR

Captain Gunn served 39 years as a TWA pilot with more than 36 years as Captain. He has flown most all transport models from the DC-3, DC-4, Martin 202-404, all Lockheed Constellations plus L-12A and C-60 Loadstar, Convair 880, Boeing 707/720, L-1011, closing his career with eleven enjoyable years on the Jumbo Boeing 747. He has over 28,000 hours of flying, which included more than 1,000 ocean crossings. He served as a flight instructor, line check pilot, Supervisor of Flight Operations (Staff), and Supervisor pilot to Saudia Airlines. He flew Pacific Military Airlift Command to Southeast Asia in 1966-68, including a White House Press Charter to the Southeast Asia Conference with President Johnson in 1966. He has held positions on the Air Line Pilot's Association committees for Training, Safety, and Aeromedicine.

Dr. Gunn received B.A. and M.A degrees in Psychology at University of Missouri-Kansas City in 1960-63. He served as psychologist on the staff of the Kansas University Medical Center Children's Rehabilitation Unit from 1963-66. While flying, he continued postgraduate studies and conducted research of genetic factors in alcoholism while an assistant clinical professor of psychiatry at KUMC and completed his doctoral studies and dissertation on the "Aeromedical Aspects of Alcoholism" in 1981.

He has written numerous aviation articles on human factors, aviation psychology, and flight safety policies and procedures. Four research studies have been accepted by major psychology and psychiatric journals. Since retirement from airline flying, he has conducted programs in wellness, stress management, and aerophobia at KUMC.

Additionally, Captain Gunn is Adjunct Professor of Aviation at Central Missouri State University conducting classes in aviation physiology and human factors.

INTRODUCTION

It is difficult these days to read, hear, or watch the news without getting the impression that flying the airlines is like playing Russian roulette.

Ironically, at a time when more Americans than ever are boarding the U.S. airlines, fear of flying is increasing — affecting even those who up to now have regarded commercial air transportation as safer than driving their own cars. The news media's voices of doom have created an epidemic of white knuckles.

Walt Gunn's book is a new voice, one of calm and logic. Fear of flying is the epitome of illogic in virtually every respect, spawned by lack of knowledge, misinformation and, in many cases, imbedded psychological trauma. No one is more qualified to help you overcome fear than an airline captain like Walt Gunn — as the saying goes, the first one to arrive at the scene of an accident is the guy flying the plane.

I've known Walt for years. He is a pilot's pilot, dedicated, skilled and with a deep sense of compassion for the so-called "white knuckle" set. I would fly with him anywhere, and by the same token I would listen to his words of wisdom anytime nervousness tried to overcome my common sense. Yet this book is not merely a job of hand-holding; it offers a practical road to flight-without-fear, a blueprint for enjoying air travel without needless qualms.

Follow his road map and you will come to regard flying as I have over the past four decades — the safest form of transportation known to man.

Robert J. Serling,
former aviation editor
United Press International

Preface:

The Joy Of Flying: Overcoming the FEAR!

This book is the product of two careers: flying and psychology. It has been written to help those who **dread flying** overcome their fears, but it is also intended to shed light on the problem for those who **enjoy flying,** so they may more clearly understand the anxiety and fear that others feel (friends, business associates, or loved ones, especially spouses) thus limiting the enjoyment of air travel.

A major premise which encouraged the writing of this book is the notion that a state of "learned helplessness" prevails among those who suffer unduly from a fear of flying. The goal is to counter the negative learning that led to such helplessness with knowledge, insight, optimism and confidence in managing the irrational fear and discomfort that is associated with flying.

As a retired airline pilot and now a practicing psychologist, I have had many opportunities to observe a wide range of emotional states among my airline passengers over the past four decades. None ever suspected that the pilot was a psychologist in disguise as their Captain.

When I retired from TWA after 39 years in the cockpit, another "takeoff" was called for: launching a career in psychology. New challenges came in the form of questions, especially those related to stress, anxiety, and fear of flying, and they begged for answers. Now as a pilot-psychologist, my clinical interest continues to grow in search of the many human factors related to flying.

My close observation of airline passengers since the early 1940s revealed that many air travellers do experience some overt level of apprehension while in flight. Even the more "macho types" fail, at times, to conceal their uneasiness.

For others, white knuckles and compressed lips suggest all too plainly the true state of their emotions, even during routine flying. Non-routine events reveal more obviously pained facial expressions. The large number of individuals who have these fears has been of both interest and concern to me as an airline pilot. Now, as a psychologist, I have added interest because I know that these fears can be greatly lessened, or at least controlled.

Psychologists have a name for the fear of flying. They call it **aerophobia.**

Though many studies suggest that public speaking is the dominant fear among most of us, fear of flying ranks a close second. Certain aerophobics might argue the point, since nothing offers a greater threat to them than the thought of flying, while speaking before a large audience may hold no threat at all.

Support for these observations is convincing when one considers the vast number of professional entertainers and successful business executives who dread having to fly — often limiting their careers — because of the pangs of agony they feel when flying. And yet, they manage easily to contain their anxieties when the spotlight looms and they take the stage or address an important audience.

Recently, I embarked on a course of study in order to learn more of the reasons underlying these fears. So many travellers gain such pleasure from flying — free from fear — it is disheartening that more would be passengers could not share the same pleasure.

Because of my aviation background, colleagues at the Kansas University Medical Center (KUMC) began referring clients to me who had admitted to being afraid to fly. They felt that my flying experiences and KUMC affiliation as an assistant clinical professor of psychiatry might prove helpful in resolving their clients' problems. Thus was born a program of Aerophobia Seminars at KUMC, which is a natural "blending of aviation & psychology."

As an airline Captain, I was occasionally called to the passenger cabin to assist in allaying the fears of an emotionally distraught passenger. Embarrassment usually compounded the person's fearful reactions and discomfort.

My approach to these anxious, white-knuckled passengers was simply to put them at ease. I would usually ask, "Can you do me a favor?" My question invariably brought a change in their facial expression. Fear turned to puzzlement as they always responded affirmatively, wondering, "How can I possibly help the pilot?"

I would follow with this request. "Can you wiggle your toes for me?" By now, they were completely baffled, usually staring off to a distant point as they responded, "Yes, I can." "Good," I'd reply, knowing that for the moment at least, they were distracted from their discomfort. I would then continue with a comment explaining that flexing the extremities reduces tension in the body, and it would work! They always began to relax. I was never sure why, but I never needed to question the results.

As the dialogue continued, it would become apparent that prolonging the distraction resulted in a further defusing of their dread. Once they experienced a reduction in tension, their anxiety level "melted away" and a calmer composure surfaced.

While flying, I felt my success in easing a passenger's stressful state of fear was largely a matter of "Captain's charisma." Now as a psychologist, I can identify the dynamics involved in those seemingly simple pilot-to-passenger encounters in psychological terms... along with an occasional sprinkling of insights acquired as a pilot, of course!

By including these experiences in this book, I hope "The Joy of Flying" will be a valuable asset for all who suffer from aerophobia, and will provide enlightenment for those who are closely associated with aerophobics and desire to help them. There is a distinct need for greater insight and understanding of the contributing factors in aerophobia, and to learn there are effective methods for alleviating a "dread of flying."

Today, I find my role as a pilot/psychologist to be a rewarding "constructive compromise" that fills the void left since my retirement from the 747 cockpit. The nostalgia is less numbing when the "halcyon days" of airline flying are recalled. While being separated from direct contact with anxiety-gripped passengers aloft, I find it rewarding to offer some measure of relief from (and perhaps prevention of) their irrational fears by counselling them in the Aerophobia Seminars.

For an untold number who are unable to seek relief in a similar program, I am happy to offer this book, which I trust will serve to enlighten and encourage them to take control of their undue fears and ultimately learn to enjoy the many pleasures of air travel.

I am encouraged by those who have sought counsel in overcoming their flying fears. The desire and dedication to gain control of their admittedly irrational fears have met with gratifying results in more than 80 percent of the cases.

Sharing in their success has been as rewarding as making a smooth landing in a 747 with a round of applause from passengers showing their appreciation for a safe and pleasant flight.

So, welcome aboard. Here's wishing you good reading, joyful flying, and happy landings... always!

June 1987   W.H.G.

Chapter One

THE FEAR OF FLYING (Apologies to Erica Jong)

I feel a tinge of reluctance in naming this chapter because little comparison or infringement is intended with the best-selling book, FEAR OF FLYING by author Erica Jong, which had little if anything to do with flying. Quite the contrary is the case, since Ms. Jong's treatise was sexually tantalizing while this overview of the topic is more technical than titillating.

Several million people, worldwide, fly daily on today's airlines. How many of them truly enjoy flying may never be known. The number of those who suffer fearfully while flying, but continue to fly, is also unknown. Those who avoid flight because of their fear of flying could number in the millions the world over, but their actual numbers are left to conjecture.

Fear of flying is a common, modern problem. Present estimates suggest some 25 million Americans are so afflicted. Avoiding the dread and discomfort that stem from their phobic attitudes toward flight, deprives them from enjoying the services of modern air transportation.

Families become isolated, job opportunities are missed, corporations lose key employees, and countless lives are disrupted, when air travel is unnecessarily avoided by so many.

Missed revenues, to the airlines alone, could approximate $2 billion annually. The economic impact to the industry is a secondary problem, but still a problem worth resolving.

It seems reasonable to assume that a fear of flying has been around since the time of the Wright Brothers, but there have been surprisingly few studies addressing the problem. Adequate research is nil.

One study conducted for market research some 20 years ago by the *Chicago Tribune* attempted to differentiate "air travelers from air avoiders." The sample consisted of 180 subjects, all adults, and 73 of them women. The study found that the two groups differed "psychologically" in the way they viewed air travel.

The difference was largely along "social dimensions," which suggested that air travelers were more sophisticated, intelligent, ambitious, wealthy, successful, and they usually travelled on business.

1

Air avoiders were seen as worriers, low in ambition, weak, less affluent, timid, bashful, and seldom travelled anyway. The issue of fear or safety was not mentioned or alluded to in any context. As a marketing survey, it remains a mystery to me that the researchers failed in defining those who avoided air travel because of fear. Perhaps, the wrong questions were asked!

The study concluded that "air travel has no other meaning for people except saving time." Saving time is of little interest when fear is the major concern of an aerophobic.

A later study by Dr. Marvin Aronson, a psychologist, revealed a different and more dynamic view of the problem. He saw "flying types" as outgoing, adventuresome, able to enjoy new experiences, self-confident, comfortable with self, enthusiastic, and interested in people and the world around them.

Dr. Aronson described aerophobics seen in his clinical practice as intelligent, educated, successful (upper middle income), perfectionistic, usually over 30 years of age, and demanding much of themselves. The majority of the men were professionals or executives. Women were artists, writers, decorators, models, actresses, or professionals, or, if housewives, married to men who were professionals or executives that fitted the above description — certainly an impressive profile of a clientele with a psychological concern.

One would expect such traits as these to conflict with other personality factors that Dr. Aronson found among his patients. The aerophobics were further described as having feelings of inadequacy or having failed in their lives. They were also seen as worriers about small events, being followers, not leaders, suffering general anxieties, not being in control of their own lives and feeling helpless in the hands of fate. All these traits are suggestive of passivity, timidity, low self-reliance, and questionable self-esteem.

What a contrast! While being achievers, they still had strong, chronic, underlying feelings of doubt. My experience with clients in aerophobia seminars also confirms that "high achievers" are not immune to a fear of flying.

These studies allow little comparison. They were conducted by vastly different sources sampled from vastly different populations. The newspaper survey of its readers could hardly be compared to the latter study, involving a group who sought treatment from a mental health practitioner. It is remarkable that the market survey failed to acknowledge the issue of "fear" as a possible reason for avoiding flight!

The multitude of reasons given for avoiding flying are often vague and difficult to assess, although it is known that those with a fear of flying expend great effort to **avoid flying.**

This book is for and about those who have a "phobic" fear of flying. **Aerophobia,** like other phobias, presents little difficulty in diagnosis. Aerophobics know their feelings only too well. They also know that their anguish can be avoided or lessened **as long as they choose not to fly**! They accept the self-imposed limitations that deprive them and their families from pleasures that can be had were it not for their undue fears of air travel.

Contributing factors and underlying influences that produce and intensify feelings of aerophobia are often unknown, or are mistakenly identified, even by those suffering from the disorder. Rationalizations center on their mental torments. They are certain tragedy is but a heartbeat away. They feel their hearts pounding ominously! Fear becomes an obsession. Their thoughts and feelings command **avoidance** or **escape** as their only choices to ease their discomforts.

The causes of their fears are both illusive and evasive. Aerophobics express great surprise when they discover a more "logical" or plausible basis for their fears, which most often, has little if anything to do with airplanes or flying!

Enlightenment intrigues. Demystifying the problem helps many. Identifying a disorder often lessens its impact. This might be called the "Rumpelstiltskin" effect, which is: name it and it goes away! Insight can be helpful in cutting through the vagueness of many irrational fears, but even then, it does not ensure the problem will vanish easily.

Finding the actual sources or causes of the fear of flying is extremely helpful in selecting a treatment plan for those seeking relief. Learning how to help aerophobics gain control over the irrational fear has been a challenging, but rewarding, accomplishment.

The "flight plan" for this book then, is to outline some of the factors related to the fear of flying and to detail some positive steps to overcome, or gain a better control of this fear.

Many of those who attended the seminars on aerophobia at the Kansas University Medical Center experienced an added benefit beyond a decrease in their agonizing fears. They found how important the role of attitudes and beliefs could be in their irrational dread of flying. But more so, they discovered the relationship of these attitudes to other difficulties in their daily living, and their coping skills improved considerably.

Overcoming a fear of flying is a tremendous achievement. Moreover, reducing anxiety and stress in other areas of living is equally rewarding. Apparently, gaining a reduction of stress in specific situations can yield greater benefits in general. Anxieties, fears, and stresses that are totally unrelated to flying can also be lessened by the attitude changes that are effective in overcoming a fear of flying. That's no small benefit!

The Question Of Safety

Safety records in aviation are unimpressive to aerophobics. They are well acquainted with the statistics that suggest air travel is more than 20 times safer than automobile travel. Their doubts persist though, and even when they agree with the convincing data, it provides little relief from their fear.

Insurance companies are excellent sources for data on risk factors related to any activity. It is important to note that life insurance coverage for air travel requires no added premium, not even for commercial pilots flying more than a thousand hours annually.

Aerophobics maintain a constant vigilance for tragedies involving airplanes. They become obsessed with each accident as it occurs. Unfortunately, there were a number of such tragedies in 1985, and that year concluded with a record number of fatalities worldwide: some 1,800 air accident deaths. It was obviously not a good year by the standards of previous years.

For example, consider the years 1980, 1981, and 1983. The major scheduled U. S. airlines flew nearly a billion passengers, making some 10 million takeoffs and landings — with ZERO fatalities! But this impressive mark is given little credit by those chronically fearful.

One important observation should be made about the number of fatalities recorded during 1985: fewer than 9% (166 deaths) occurred on **major scheduled U. S. airlines!** The other fatalities (over 1,600) occurred on foreign airlines, non-scheduled charter airlines, small commuters, or air taxi flights.

These deaths are certainly no less tragic, but the point needs to be made that there are vast differences in the safety records of the various airlines. Major scheduled airlines in the U.S. have consistently compiled enviable safety records — unmatched the world over!

In 1986, air safety improved on a worldwide basis, although unofficial accounts revealed nearly 500 fatalities occurred on foreign carriers. On a much more favorable note, 1986 concluded as one of commercial aviation's safest years ever in the United States. Again, there were **zero fatalities involving a major U. S. airline**!

Bob Serling, noted aviation writer, cleverly translated the risk factors, that is, the chances of ever being involved in a fatal accident as an airline passenger. He computed that you could be "born" on an airliner today and fly continuously to the age of 78 years before possibly being involved in a fatal mishap!

Lloyds of London is elated to cover such odds. But regardless, the use of logic is ineffective for alleviating the concerns of the aerophobic. As humans, we are truly creatures of our emotions — not our intellect!

Phobias In Everyday Life

Estimates of the prevalence of phobic disorders vary from expert to expert. The professional literature contains very few studies about the frequency of phobias in the general population.

Research data from the National Institute of Mental Health (NIMH) report, as mentioned earlier, found that "fear of flying" is second to the "fear of public speaking" among 11 million phobics in the U. S. Further data from the NIMH reveal:

1) Seven percent of the population or about 11 million persons in the U.S. require treatment for a phobia of some sort in any six-month period;

2) One in nine adults suffers some form of phobic disorder, and of these, one in 20 involves agoraphobia, a disabling fear of leaving home and dread of public places.

Other studies provide a variety of data describing other factors known about phobias.

For example, a Vermont survey conducted in 1969 concluded that perhaps eight percent of the general population suffer some type of phobia that will interfere with their daily living.

Additionally, among psychiatric patients diagnosed with mental or emotional disorders, phobias are present in 20 to 44 percent.

A study of subjects in New Haven, Conn., Baltimore, Md., and St. Louis, Mo., yielded further general data:

1) For women, phobias were the most common disorder in the 18 to 65 year age group. In general, three times more women than men suffer phobias. It is heartening to note the rate of phobias lowers for both men and women after age 65 (a result of learning or conditioning?).

2) For men, phobias ranked third in the 18-24 year age group, behind alcohol abuse and drug abuse/dependency. Phobias advanced to second place from age 25 to 65, behind alcohol abuse/dependence.

Accurate data on phobic disorders are difficult to come by for a variety of reasons. Surveys such as those above are random samplings of limited populations. Furthermore, not all persons seek treatment for the same reasons, and some never seek counsel or help at all. And too, many may be acceptant of their irrational fears.

Phobias that appear before the age of 20 tend to fade and disappear with lessening consequence. Onsets after adolescence last longer, and in one-third become more severe, with marked impairment in 20 percent. After age 40, disabling fears are frequently associated with an illness or depression.

In the case of aerophobia, there is room for skepticism about women exceeding men by a three or four-to-one ratio. Because of the reluctance of some men to admit their fears or to seek help, there is a potential for inaccuracy in the data.

In our culture, men frequently assume a macho role that masks their fears. Men are more resistant than women to seeing their problems as psychological, as attested to by the lower incidence of men who consult mental health professionals. Men appear to have less fear of losing self-control than do women, but men are more concerned when they are not in control of situations, such as when flying as a passenger.

What are the numbers of men who avoid flying because of fear but disguise their reasons? How many men fly, but do so on the "edge of panic," inwardly struggling to maintain an outward coolness? We'll never know, but the numbers might be astounding.

The possibilities exist that there is a significant number of men who are fearful of flying, but who will not seek relief, for fear of revealing their frailty.

Enrollment in our Aerophobia Seminars also has had a three-to-one ratio, with men in the minority. Success rates of both are similar: 75 to 80 percent show "some positive gain" in flying with a lowered level of anxiety or fear.

Of those with a remaining concern, the men sustain a greater measure of uneasiness and "disabling doubt." Dread nullifies their projecting a macho image. Lessening their discomfort is a slower process, but the reasons are difficult to determine; explanations are largely conjectures.

Need for authority appears to be a greater problem for men. The authoritarian role is manifested by traits which demand obedience from others and a more strict adherence to orderly processes. Not being in command or control is disconcerting or frustrating to a patriarch, or perhaps to a matriarch, with similarly disturbing consequences.

The authoritarians' problems with aerophobia are not resolved easily. There must be an attitudinal change, which involves granting authority to others they may hold in lesser esteem. Rigid authoritative attitudes intensify anxieties when such "leader types" are forced into a more **passive** role. **Forced passivity is frustrating and irritability often results**! Anxiety escalates! In fact, for many, anxiety leads to irritability, and being irritable often leads to **depression**. Depression is frequently a major symptom of the phobias.

It is this formulation that best describes those who suffer from not being in control of conditions affecting them.

Adherence to the authority of others prevails in the world of travel. Rules and regulations are enforced by bus drivers, train clerks, baggage handlers, flight attendants, and pilots; all of them expect the travelling public to adhere to their sometimes irritating mandates.

When major personality factors are accurately assessed and considered, overcoming an irrational fear of flying is possible, but total victory should not be expected. Regardless, four out of five of those who have come forward seeking relief in a treatment program succeed in becoming more comfortable and able to tolerate flying with less discomfort.

The ultimate challenge must be met by actually flying. A group flight led by a therapist has proved quite helpful. Also, flying with a spouse or close friend who has attended the program can offer supportive encouragement that is timely and beneficial. Without flying, the continued avoidance must be seen as failure!

Whatever the basis of the phobic discomfort, it can be dissolved, and once frightened persons succeed in flying with less fear, the contentment that is felt as they gain "freedom from fear" is its own reward.

Robert Burton writing in *The Anatomy of Melancholy* aptly states:

"They that live in fear are never free." His observation is so true, and freedom is a most prized possession for mankind.

Chapter 2

THIS IS YOUR CAPTAIN SPEAKING

The technical training of airline pilots is intensive and complex. Human behavior is not addressed nor is it deemed to be relevant to the performance of a pilot's normal duties.

My first encounters with aerophobics occurred during my early years as a pilot for TRANS WORLD AIRLINES, long before I had any training as a psychologist. Our flight hostesses (now called flight attendants) were selected for their expertise in attending to those passengers who showed varying degrees of anxiety during a flight. In fact, the earliest hostesses were required to be registered nurses to provide more "professional" care for the passengers. On occasions, I was called to help calm a frightened passenger, only to add to the TLC already in progress.

I soon learned there is no simple way to classify aerophobics. At times, all types of passengers from all walks of life suffer fearfully while flying. Both men and women are afflicted, but more women than men seek help for their uncontrollable, discomforting fear of flying.

The expression of fear varies. Many suffer quietly in their anguish; others react hysterically. Some "tough it out" unaided, while others fly with the support of pills or with a few, stiff, alcoholic drinks for quick fixes, all of which are largely ineffective for long-term relief.

For some, the mere thought of flying grips them with sheer panic. Anticipating a trip by air is agonizing. Obsessions overwhelm. Avoiding flight is their only solution, but avoidance only intensifies the fear when there is a need (or desire) to fly.

During my early years of airline flying (before graduate study in psychology), I tried to use compassion and empathy to reassure any jittery passengers. But, more than likely, the authoritarian image of Captain was the most effective factor in calming an anxious, panicky passenger. I must confess that initially I had no thought-out system. I simply used what seemed to work, and it always did.

Passengers were always grateful, but I remained curious about what **really** took place in alleviating their fear.

One of the first things I learned about aerophobia is that even "tough guys" are not immune. In fact, one of the fearful passengers I remember most vividly was a Hollywood actor, well-known for his macho-tough image in gangster roles. The incident is still amusing to recall:

9

It was a sweltering summer evening, and I was about to board my DC-3 in Wichita, enroute to Amarillo. The hostess requested that I meet this famous actor, but not for any "fan talk" of his past movies, nor for his autograph, nor for social niceties. There was a problem.

From the cabin door, I saw this robust, hero-type actor standing at the base of the loading steps; he was frenzied, visibly grimacing, and reluctant to board the plane.

As I approached him on the ramp he pleaded "Don't take off!" Somehow he had spotted lightning flashes to the west and had become terrified at the thought of flying into the storms.

I assured him by saying, "There's no reason to be concerned about the lightning. The weather is to the north of our course." Smiling, I went on, "I don't like storms either, but it will be easy to avoid these. Come on and we'll enjoy the firework display together — from a safe distance." (I never used the term 'lightning' when speaking with passengers. The term 'static discharge' is a much more palatable term and 'rain showers' is much preferred to 'thunderstorms.' There are many less threatening terms that pilots prefer to use with their passengers.)

This popular movie star's predicament intrigued me. Somehow, I felt other factors were involved. This veteran actor, fearless on screen, was enjoying his performance as though he had an audience, which he did have!

In those earlier days of air travel, a favorite pastime for the prairie-bound citizens of Wichita was to go to the airport to watch the planes and occasionally see a famous passenger. On this evening 100 or more plane-watching spectators, behind a fence some 50 feet from our DC-3, were in open view of this dramatic performance of human anguish.

At that moment, I knew I had to counter with a diversion, lest the scene go on and on. The time for takeoff was approaching, so I moved in on the problem. I mentioned one of his roles in which he met his demise — by setting his jaw and marching resolutely into blazing gunfire — brave as Hell! He grinned. I had him! Vanity overwhelmed his anxiety.

I continued, and asked if he would do me a favor. It's hard to deny the Captain, so he agreed. I then asked (more like commanded) him to come on board, assuring him that we would "ride this out together" with absolute safety.

He hesitated. I then added, nonchalantly, "If you don't, we'll have to remove your luggage and let you wait until the weather clears tomorrow." He studied his options while trying to negotiate further, but to no avail. Finally, stretching his stocky stature he marched up the loading steps.

There was a sprinkling of applause and a few muffled cheers as he gestured to his audience. He left his "stage" and swaggered into the plane to further applause from the passengers waiting on board.

We left and our flight proved uneventful. I visited with him after we landed safely and he was gracious in his praise for such a pleasant flight. He had rested well, perhaps pleased with his brief performance. Apparently gaining attention from his suffering was rewarding. In psychology, we call this **secondary gain,** a situation in which individuals gain attention or sympathy from their discomfort. Children know this ploy well, and maturity does not signal the end of such behavioral strategies! Maybe immaturity lingers with hero-type actors as well.

Subsequently, I viewed his screen performances with a greater appreciation of his acting skills when he portrayed a villainous, tough-guy image since I knew him to be a gentle, sensitive man capable of fear, much unlike his acting roles.

After observing fearful passengers for a decade as a pilot, I entered graduate studies in clinical psychology at the University of Missouri in Kansas City (UMKC). My major interest was in human engineering, a sub-topic in psychology. Since then, those years of study served to broaden my insight into the vagaries of human behavior.

For one thing, I noticed that many anxious passengers come up with their own systems to make flying tolerable, if not enjoyable.

For example, a popular **Tonight Show** comedian is well-known as a "nervous flyer," as are many famous funny men. Somehow this performer learned a basic principle of stress management: **Activity Absorbs Anxiety.** (It really does!)

He ambles up and down the aisles during his frequent 747 flights back and forth to Los Angeles. (747s are like hotel lobbies, with ample room for strolling.)

During such a flight I toured the cabin and casually asked the strolling comic, "Where are you going?" I was merely being friendly, by making a passenger relations visit with idle chit-chat, so I thought.

The comic leaped at my words and replied, "Hey, that's funny! Here we are, 35,000 feet in the air and the Captain asks me where I'm going." His captive audience broke into laughter. Revelry spread throughout the cabin (such live entertainment in flight is a rare treat). His antics were relaxing for all, which confirms an axiom in the psychology of humor: **Laughter Relieves Stress!**

Later, I watched him on the **Tonight Show,** and he used this vignette in one of his comedy routines. For him, physical activity plus his humor makes flying much easier to endure. There's a message here for others as well. Humor is an excellent antidote for anxiety, as Norman Cousins concludes when he suggests using laughter as therapy for the stress of the seriously ill (more on this in Chapter 6).

Regardless of their self-assured images, many prominent athletes are not immune to aerophobia. In the 1950s I was assigned to fly a major league baseball team on a charter flight. Secretly, I enjoyed flying sports charters. An early interest in baseball was revived when I met with past or future "Hall of Famers." Autographed baseballs from famous athletes among my passengers were treasured mementos for my two sons, Tim and Rick.

On this particular trip, I greeted some of the players in the gate area to chat briefly with them. I was well aware that many professional athletes are apprehensive about flying. Knowing that, I felt that being more personable and visiting with the teams would help. After all, it worked well with others and airline management encouraged the cockpit crews to be more personalized in "passenger contact" when their duties allowed such socializing.

After takeoff, it dawned on me that one of the team members, a real "super star," was missing. I hadn't heard that he was on the disabled list, and certainly, the team would never trade him. His absence was puzzling.

On charter flights (and before high-jacking) I would usually keep the cockpit door open, allowing passengers to visit if they were interested. Shortly after takeoff, one team member entered the cockpit to look around, which gave me a chance to inquire about the missing player. His teammate said he was driving to the game — some 1100 miles! In fact, he **never** travelled by air. I had never heard that he was aerophobic, and it aroused my curiosity. Why was such an excellent athlete frozen with such fear? I still wonder.

The outcome of this story is disheartening. A year later, when the leagues expanded to the West Coast, this superb athlete voluntarily quit baseball, midway in his illustrious career! Ground travel coast-to-coast, overnight, was impossible. His inability to fly left him little option to meet the heavy playing schedule. What a loss of talent! Surely, I felt, some form of treatment could have saved his career.

Since then, I have become more aware that this was not an isolated case. Many skilled and high-performing individuals suffer the same affliction. How many is not known, although numerous corporations are known to provide counselling for key personnel to help them overcome problems with flying. I am confident that everyone benefits when a career is saved.

On the other hand, John Madden, former coach of the then Oakland Raiders and now a sports commentator, profits well from his aerophobic capers. Commercials for a popular beer company find him in a train club car asserting, ''Me, afraid of flying? I'm not afraid of anything!'' At that moment the train enters a darkened tunnel. When it emerges, Big John Madden is cowering under a table, apparently fearful of the darkness — or tunnels — or both!

No doubt, he profits handsomely from these commercials. He has little incentive to overcome his fear of flying as long as he is able to capitalize on his dread, with humor. Few aerophobics are as fortunate as John Madden.

Another fascinating incident occurred on a later flight after completing graduate study in psychology. Passengers had boarded the International 747 at a gate some distance from the main terminal. They were driven to the airplane on a mobile lounge, a bus-like device. When the lounge returned to the terminal the passengers were stranded from the gate areas. A feeling of isolation grew among the passengers as an unexplained delay was encountered. In such situations, it is not unusual for apprehension to build into feelings of anxiety, even fear, in some of the passengers.

Meanwhile, the purser, Jon Proctor, summoned me on the interphone and requested that I come down to the cabin (the cockpit on the 747 is on an upper deck above the passengers' cabin) to assist in calming a young lady near panic. She was pleading desperately to leave the airplane.

I made my way to the cabin and as I approached her, it was clear that she indeed appeared to be on the verge of losing her self-control.

My distraction gambit was called for. Grinning, I made the familiar request and asked her for a favor — the toe wiggle challenge. With a puzzled expression, she glanced down at her feet and we both noted the flexing movement. I then went on, saying, "That's fine. Now I know you can relax, because if you can flex your toes, you can't remain tense, and you are more relaxed now, aren't you?" She agreed, but held a dubious look as she pondered my request. The purser studied the transaction from behind the young lady's seat.

As we chatted, she appeared to regain her composure, when suddenly she blurted, "But my batteries are dead!" Such a tangential remark as this had a distinct flavor of schizophrenia! Was it possible that she was out of contact with reality? If so, my "band-aid" manner of dealing with a psychosis was destined to fail.

A more clinical approach was considered for the moment, when much to my relief, she clarified her apparent non sequitur remark. She had flown in from the West Coast where she had seen a therapist for her fear of flying. He had given her a cassette tape to induce relaxation for her upcoming trip to Europe. (I include such a tape in my seminars, or as a mail order item.)

In her trip from California, she had used the cassette, and now, the batteries were depleted! Her anxiety had peaked. Her dilemma now was — facing a six-hour panic-packed flight across the Atlantic without the consoling commentary of her therapist! She felt abandoned without it. Anxiety flooded her every thought.

I assured her that I would try to locate batteries, but first, I suggested that she might try something for me. It was apparent that she was open to help and change since the recorded message on the tape had been effective in soothing her frenzied fear this far.

I suggested, "Try my smile, breathe, relax, exercise." Leading her, I smiled. She smiled. Then, exaggerating my gestures, I inhaled. She mimicked me. Slowly exhaling, I drooped my shoulders. She slumped softly in her seat, visibly relaxed and at ease. She was responding well to each cue; the distraction was making successful inroads on her tensely anxious state.

I continued to talk to her about the importance of learning relaxation techniques and using them whenever she felt tense or anxious. She remained attentive and continued with the slowed breathing, while becoming more relaxed.

Again, I spoke softly asking her to "follow me and breathe deeply... slowly, exhale... now close your eyes as we relax... deeper... that's good!" Her eyes remained gently closed, her facial muscles slackened into a soft smile.

I went on. "Now, during flight, it helps to learn to relax by feeling **heavy** in your seat. Just relax, sink deeper, let the seat support you fully. Now, feel the **warmth** coming over your whole body. Let it flow through your arms... your legs... feeling very comfortable, relaxed, **heavy and warm**. It feels good... you're doing fine!" I waited in silence as her calm continued.

Her breathing became more natural, so I went on, saying, "breathe easily and feel the calming sensation, comfortably, pleasantly, relaxed, as you are right now. That's nice. You're doing well. Continue... and you do feel much more at ease... and you can do this anytime now that you feel tense or anxious... you're just fine... good!"

While my purser friend continued to study the proceedings, I asked the young lady to look at me, which she did with a ghost of a smile. She had recaptured the calmness that she had lost, and did so without the aid of the tape to guide her. In but a few, calming minutes, she progressed from toe wiggling to a smiling, relaxed composure. Relief spread over her, radiating unmistakably in her facial expression.

I praised her achievement and offered reassurance that she could maintain her calm control by simply remembering to **smile, breathe and relax** whenever she felt tense or anxious. Her smile broadened as she chuckled, "I'm OK now!"

I returned to the cockpit for the takeoff. It was just five hours and forty-four minutes to Madrid, and with the favorable winds forecasted, the delay would not affect an on-time arrival for breakfast in Spain.

A couple of hours into our flight, I returned to the cabin and the formerly distraught passenger was dozing restfully with not a sign of discomfort. The forced weaning from the taped message (because of the dead batteries) took no further toll on her emotionally. We never found any batteries, but by then, they weren't needed.

Afterward, Jon, my purser colleague, commented that he was curious about the unusual episode that he had witnessed. He asked for a tape of the relaxation technique for his future use. I assured him that he could be as effective with his "own style" for comforting uneasy passengers. His casual charm was infectious enough to comfort his passengers. He needed only to know the basics: make them smile, breathe and relax, gently urging them in his usual consoling manner. Suggesting they feel heavy and warm would add to the assurance that relaxation will occur. With Jon's affable nature, little else would be needed.

I am continually astonished at the number of world-renowned persons who have an aversion to flying. In a recent national news publication, I read with amazement of famed leaders in the fields of science, industry, politics, and the arts who avoid air travel religiously.

The wealth of intellect among many apprehensive air travellers is impressive. To learn that Isaac Asimov, award winning science fiction author, chooses not to fly, is a puzzling paradox. I pondered over what likely reasons he might give for objecting to conventional flight as a means of safe and convenient transportation, but I was always left with more questions than answers.

Then, on a recent talk show, Azimov declared that he was an "incurable acrophobe," suggesting that he sees his dread of flight a result of his fear of heights. As an "incurable optimist," I am confident there are answers for acrophobes as well as aerophobes, and that acrophobia need not predispose one to being aerophobic! Moreover, fear of heights is a negligible factor among those attending the seminars. (further discussion of acrophobia is in Chapter 4 and Chapter 7, involving Carl)

Fear is a human experience that we all share with varying reactions, which seems merely to be part of the essence of "being human."

These anecdotes about well-known persons should underscore the idea that aerophobia can be a problem for anyone, even the strong, rich, or famous. Nevertheless, most of the hundreds of aerophobics I have known, both as a pilot and as a psychologist, have been ordinary individuals just like you and me.

In earlier flying days, flight crews were notified when "first flyers" boarded the airplane. Extra attention was given to put them at ease. There was a more intimate bond between the pilot and passengers, which is often lacking with the mass numbers on today's jumbo-sized planes. Unfortunately, air travel has become more impersonal.

After becoming a psychologist, there was little need for change in my "modus operandi" with passengers. While in flight, the so-called "Captain's charisma" is undoubtedly as effective as any psychologist's plan for arresting a fear of flying.

There is really no need for special psychology courses in the training programs for airline pilots. Captain training is intensive in setting forth the principles of "command authority and responsibility," and it suffices in maintaining a safe and orderly operation, especially during emergencies.

For example, 'SCD' is a term familiar to most airline employees; it stands for 'Subject Captain's Discretion,' which makes it implicit that tactful judgment is to be expected in all command decisions.

Pilots revere the SCD philosophy. When it comes to unusual situations not covered by the exhausting array of federal air regulations or company policies and procedures, the most bizarre happenings can be resolved with confidence as long as tactful discretion is the pilot's guideline.

The effectiveness of my fellow pilots in managing passenger problems is impressive, and I know of none who is also a trained professional psychologist.

Professionalism in all matters involving the safety of passengers, crew and aircraft is emphasized throughout the Captain training program. Pilots live by the SCD principle and it serves them and their passengers well.

The most illuminating example of command discretion was observed world-wide during the TWA Flight 847 incident, under the command of Captain John Testrake as he dealt with the highly-publicized, terrorist incident in Beirut.

Amid the accolades given him after concluding the stressful encounter, Captain Testrake denied any heroism on his part by stating humbly, "I did little that any other TWA Captain would not have done, given the same situation."

John praised his early Captain training course with TWA while he assigned equal credit to his confidence in the abilities of his flight crew members who demonstrated responsible concern for the safety and needs of their passengers.

Uli Dericksen, purser on·Captain Testrake's flight, was truly dedicated in her concern for the safety and well-being of her passengers. Although she thrust her body in front of a gunman intending to execute one of her passengers who was held hostage, she shuns the role of heroine! Not heroic?

John Testrake and Uli Dericksen epitomize the level of professionalism and discretional concern that airline crews have for their passengers. Universally, the air transport industry takes great pride in maintaining the traditions of public concern for air travellers that has prevailed since the infancy of commercial flying. I could not feel any greater personal pride than I have in being a part of an industry that has such humanistic concern for others. Indeed, I am confident, you are in good hands!

Chapter 3

THIS IS YOUR PSYCHOLOGIST SPEAKING

*Control over thought is a long, painful, and
laborious process. But I am convinced that
no time, no labor, and no pain is too much for
the glorious result to be reached.*

Harmony of Body and Mind — Gandhi

After some fifteen years of airline piloting and with my increasing a interest in space research in the late 1950s, I developed a concern for the human factors in aviation. "Human engineering" was a sub-specialty in psychology which considers the human elements, physically and emotionally. It then made sense to me to pursue graduate study in psychology with concentration on the human factors.

Airline pilots possess a wealth of talent beyond their piloting skills. Many are also lawyers, engineers, CPAs or business majors. Among my pilot colleagues were a dentist, a veterinarian, an optometrist, and several professional athletes including a golfer of some note, a veritable wealth of diverse talent and resources. There were un-doubtedly many psychology majors among the pilots, but to my knowledge, none was a trained psychologist.

I felt there was a need for experienced pilots with formal training in the behavioral sciences — as much as the physical sciences — to address the human element in aviation. There should be no doubt that human factors are intricately interwoven with mechanical factors (and design) that can seriously affect flight safety.

In the young aviation industry with limited financial resources, when economy was an issue, human engineering was forced to give way to the mechanical factors involved in structural design, performance, and available technologies. Those with a concern for the human element met with considerable frustration.

Early aircraft design followed the principle that "man fit the machine," which violated many of the basic elements of human function and physical limitations. Reaching man's limitations created a serious compromise with safety. Advocacy for the human aspect was mandated when the industry developed new aircraft designs and operating procedures. The need persisted to consider the designing of "machines that fit man!"

Early design technologies lagged, which also limited the pilots' performances. Transport airplanes such as the DC-3 and DC-4 evolved on the principle requiring man to fit the machine, and many of these early transports remain in service today, still with their multitude of shortcomings.

As an example, cockpit designs provided little comfort; fatigue was often an overlooked factor; instruments were primitive; flight control forces (lacking "power steering-like" help) increased with the size of the airplane, which at times, required the physical strength of a "farm hand!"

Pilots sensed a need for change. In the 1950s, interest in human engineering reached crusade-like proportions, which prompted my return to graduate school, with focus on the human factors in aviation.

The advent of jet aircraft design and technology brought welcome change in the many short-comings. The aviation industry recognized the importance of human engineering and redirected research of the human factor to be incorporated in the jet-age transports.

Much of the graduate study in clinical psychology in the 1960s was based on Freudian psychoanalytical theory. These views of human behavior were heavily weighted with the importance of the "sex drive." Phobias (and assuredly aerophobia) were seen as a consequence of frustrations, fixations, conflicts, or some form of sexual "hangup."

Using Freudian symbolism, intriguing tales could be spun to explain a human beings' complex behaviors as consequences of disturbances in early psychosexual development that would affect later adjustment in life.

In those days, symbolism ran rampant in assigning sexual connotations to almost everything, including inanimate objects. The breast and penis were popularly symbolized even in nature. Cloud formations were labelled "mammatus" because of their bulbous, breast-like, mammary shape. Mountain peaks were described as having a penis-like configuration; volcanic peaks titillated the imagination, especially when they erupted. In dreams and in the unconscious, birds were a phallic symbol. Surely, the tubular design of airplanes were suggestively shaped resembling the male phallus.

The sex drive served as a prime determinant of human behavior in Freud's judgment. All social interactions were seen as some manifestation of sexual encounters. Even flying could be viewed as sublimations of unconscious libidinal urges "a la Freud."

The act of flying encompasses ritualistic activities that call for examining, "even fondling" the plane prior to flight, tantamount to the act of **foreplay!** The takeoff excites a "surge of adrenaline" in many flyers, reminiscent of the moment of **"penetration,"** albeit, of the atmosphere! Cruising to destination is defined by pilots as their **"endurance"** which is determined by the amount of fuel available for the flight! Certainly, it is not difficult to view the landing as the **"climax,"** which for many flyers is a near-orgasmic event!

The joy of flying may not be as exhilarating as the sexual encounter, although I've never known a pilot who didn't enjoy "making landings!" A vicarious thrill perhaps, but orgasmic? I'm dubious!

But then, what about the aerophobic? Could not an irrational fear of flying be symptomatic of some form of sexual dysfunction? (Freudian analysts might support such a notion.)

If so, treatment may best be relegated to a sex therapist rather than to a pilot/psychologist. (Rest easily; I have difficulty in buying this theory.)

A more pragmatic approach satisfies my clinical view of the fear of flying. Changes in the behavioral sciences emerged as a result of research by **learning** theorists and **behavioral** scientists. Behaviorists modified many Freudian concepts and discounted many as little more than unverifiable hypotheses.

The fantasy-like tales spun by Freudian analysis gave way to the research of more testable theories of learning and behavior. Libido as related to flying is given little, if any, credibility.

Aerophobia Defined

According to Dr. Donald Goodwin, psychiatrist and author of *Phobia: The Facts,* there are four essential elements in any phobia. The fear must:

1) be persistent and excessive,
2) encourage avoidance,
3) be unreasonable, and
4) be disabling.

These four features must prevail to some degree, as the criteria of a phobic disorder.

Aerophobia is an irrational fear of flying that meets Dr. Goodwin's criteria when a person is confronted with the need for expedient travel, which is best served by flying, but is avoided unreasonably.

Phobias are classified as neuroses. Neurotics are intolerably convinced they are "crazy" when in fact they are not. Psychotics, on the other hand, are often "out of contact with reality" but are seldom aware they are. Neurotics are overly sensitive to reality and it frightens them. Fear overwhelms!

Both ANXIETY and FEAR are interwoven in the fabric of the neuroses, especially in the phobic disorders. To understand aerophobia more clearly, consider the following definitions.

ANXIETY — the distress or uneasiness of mind, usually produced by the perceived apprehension of danger or misfortune, the source of which is obscure or unknown. Physical symptoms accompany both the acute and the chronic states of anxiety.

Normal worry differs from anxiety. Anxiety interferes with the quality of life and when anxiety is severe, it adversely affects a person's ability to function normally. Anxiety reflects the mind-body workings and has achieved recognition as the number one mental health problem in America today!

FEAR — a distressing emotion aroused by impending pain, danger, or evil, whether real or imagined. It is the feeling or condition of being afraid of a known or suspected source. Fear is a form of "learned pain" and is often mistaken for anxiety as a means of explaining any vague feeling of uneasiness.

STRESS — a physical, chemical, or emotional factor that causes physical or mental tension, and which may be a factor in the cause of disease. Generically speaking, stress may be the physical or emotional responses (of the body) to the demands of external influences. Emotional stress may be likened to the physical concept of strain. (unfortunately, arguments abound regarding most attempts to define stress.)

ATTITUDE — a rather persistent tendency to react in a positive (favorably) or negative (unfavorably) manner to situations and to others. Attitudes are directed by our preferences and aversions related to our experiences. Change is extremely difficult. Unrealistic attitudes feed the emotions and anxiety exaggerates the emotional response.

EMOTION — a complex state of feelings, responses, and motivation most observable when aroused. Many psychologists see emotions as responses to bodily changes in heart rate and respiration. Emotions are often expressed physically by facial, vocal, or postural gestures.

PHOBIA — a persistent, excessive, unreasonable fear of a specific object, activity, or situation that results in a compelling desire to AVOID the dreaded object, activity or situation. Objects are easier to avoid than are certain situations or events. Often, the feared condition is admittedly harmless, but the fear reactions remain.

According to the psychiatric diagnostic manual, there are three classifications of phobias: **simple, social** and **agoraphobia.**

SIMPLE PHOBIAS involve a persistent, irrational fear of and compelling desire to avoid an object or situation. Phobic reactions are confined to single objects, usually animals. Phobic situations more often involve heights and closed places. Fear of heights, surprisingly as it may appear, is of lesser importance in aerophobia than I once considered, whereas claustrophobia, a fear of closed spaces or confinement time-wise, is a major concern among a significant number of the clients in the seminars.

SOCIAL PHOBIAS are similar to simple phobias in terms of persistence and avoidance. Involved are such social concerns as being scrutinized by others in public and a fear of being humiliated or embarrassed by one's own actions or conduct. A distinct majority of those in the seminars would meet the criteria for social phobia, leading me to suspect that "fear of flying is not a simple phobia" Social factors are strong determinants in sensitizing many who fear air travel.

AGORAPHOBIA is a more serious disorder wherein the individual has a marked fear of and avoids being alone in public places. The fear stems from "anticipating" that help would not be available in case of a sudden incapacitation (as in having a panic attack).

In agoraphobia, one severely constricts normal activities, and in many cases becomes "housebound" and depressed. The individual is "hostage to self-generated fears," and agitation may mask the resulting depression. The sanctuary of the home limits venturing any distance, and flying is unthinkable. Such self isolation merely aggravates and deepens the existing depression.

Aerophobia: A Social Phobia?

Many text books classify the fear of flying as a simple phobia. I disagree. My experience with participants in the seminars supports a classification of aerophobia as a social phobia. Here's an example to support this viewpoint.

Diane attended a seminar a few months in advance of taking a lengthy flight to the South Pacific. After the seminar, she felt sufficiently confident to carry out the planned trip, — but with medication for her anticipated anxiety. The flying was tolerated with surprising ease.

Diane was elated, though she felt that her success was more a credit to the medication than a result of applying the techniques learned at the seminar. When she reported to me afterwards, I detected a "tinge of guilt" in her voice as she explained her use of a medical crutch. I praised her accomplishment and assured her that the victory was justly hers, which eased her conscience.

Following the commercial airline flight, Diane had occasion to fly with her pilot husband on a business trip in a small 4-place private plane. She felt some apprehension but agreed to join him since she could call on the medication to insure her composure.

Diane opted to defer taking the anti-anxiety pill before the flight, but she kept it close at hand, just in case.

The outcome? All went well, even in some choppy air which had always ignited fear in her. Diane managed her uneasiness, and this time drug free!

The joy of conquering her fear was even more appreciated by her husband, although both overlooked an important difference in the two flights. The **social difference** was an important clue to the source of Diane's symptoms. For Diane, anxiety and fear were more intense when she felt threatened by social embarrassment. A panic attack in public would be unbearable, while flying with her husband — even in a small plane — held less threat for her. Diane agreed that her aerophobia was secondary to her fear of **public scrutiny.** Her concerns of commercial air travel are best termed a social phobia, which is indeed the case with many of those attending the seminars.

Spouses are not always effective in supporting their mates in overcoming emotional problems. In fact, marital discord is frequently a contributor to many emotional disorders. If a spouse exerts pressure to take part in a feared activity, it often intensifies the problem.

To what extent marital conflict contributes to aerophobia is unknown. Regardless, coercion or over-concern on the part of a husband or wife can be obstructive, and when such pressure is evidenced, any lessening of emotional upset is tenuous at best. There were a number of situations in the seminars when a marriage counsellor may have been more helpful in serving the needs of a participant than a pilot/psychologist could. Here's an example.

An attractive woman client (34 years old) told of an anguishing flying experience three years earlier. She had been unable to fly since.

When describing the flight, she commented that there was considerable "bouncing around," and they had to land at an alternate airport before "finally getting home." When asked how others on the flight reacted, she observed that it was not nearly so disturbing for them. When I asked what else might have occurred at the time, she stared off pensively for a moment, then casually stated, "Come to think of it, that was the time my husband and I discussed a divorce," as though the frightening flight and marital strife had little relevance!

It was easier to attribute her anguish to flying rather than to other extraneous factors (in this case the marital conflict) that were painfully associated with air travel, and which were obviously repressed.

Her husband had played an unwitting role in contributing to the acquired discomfort, and support from him therefore, would be unlikely. She attended the seminar alone and did well. Some fare better in overcoming their fears with support from those who are emotionally neutral, rather than with an involved family member. The seminar served her needs, and the threat of flying was greatly diminished. At last account, the marriage survived.

Fear Or Phobia?

A phobia is best described as an excessive fear in the absence of real danger. Other dimensions are useful in determining when fear becomes a phobia.

Fear should be rational. Phobias are irrational and often exaggerated forms of fear. Anxiety is a by-product of both, and feelings of insecurity flourish; undetected depression often results.

Phobias complicate our lives, especially when avoidance is not an option. Anxiety may range from mild uneasiness to a crippling disability, depending on the extent of the perceived threat to the person.

Phobic reactions create a form of "anxiety neurosis." While phobias are considered neurotic, they are not terminal. They are treatable with a good prognosis for improvement! In fact, most phobias are considered benign with little need for treatment, as long as they don't interfere with routine activities in a normally pursued way of life.

For example, a fear of snakes should be of minimal concern to city dwellers, whereas others who fear snakes must take precaution if they are to enjoy country outings.

Phobic disorders, unlike more serious illnesses or diseases, will often subside after treatment of the symptoms alone. The prognosis is encouraging with a variety of treatments. Seeking counsel is beneficial, even mandatory, when the phobia interferes with a person's enjoyment in living, or restricts a normal life style.

Fear Or Anxiety?

Fear strikes when danger is sensed; anxiety disturbs when uneasiness is felt. Both emotions are unpleasant.

Fear and anxiety are superficially similar, but there is an essential difference. We are fearful of a **known** object or situation. We are anxious, of what, we **know not.** Fear is specific. Anxiety is general and diffuse. Fear produces anxiety, but being anxious need not make us fearful.

In a fearful state, irrational thought leads to erratic behavior. Confusion is common. Decision-making is impaired. Problem-solving is difficult for a person who is either fearful or anxious. When either fear or anxiety becomes irrationally excessive, a phobia is born!

Anxiety disorders have recently come to the fore of public recognition as the number one mental health problem today for women, and the number two problem for men (after drug and alcohol abuse, which may well result from attempts to escape anxiety!).

Anxiety is a central symptom in the phobias. Even for non- phobics, anxiety prevails as part and parcel of the human experience. Anxiety is a general response of the nervous system which serves to alert the body to a potential threat. Man's concealed vulnerabilities are unmasked by his anxieties.

Early psychoanalysis saw anxiety as a consequence of the "birth trauma" process. Universal anxiety resulted from the radical transition from womb to the external world: something all humans are forced to endure in the birth encounter -- some with less difficulty than others.

While the various views of the origin of anxiety are but conjectures that are difficult to prove, they are equally difficult to disprove. The study of behavior remains an inexact science, and certainly an art.

Nevertheless, we are left with a greater mystery. Why does anxiety differ so widely from one person to another? Vast differences are noted among individuals reacting to the same situations. Studies support genetic influences in the emotional disorders. A person's anxiety attacks increase significantly if a biological relative (especially an identical twin) shows signs of an anxiety disorder. Genetic research continues.

Chronic anxiety is depressing, which compounds the discomfort and complicates the treatment process. Most often, antidepressant medication is the choice of physicians in treating phobic disorders. Agoraphobia responds well when medical management is directed to an underlying depression.

Anxiety may be seen as both a **symptom** and a **response** (or cause) in the neurotic disorders. Physiological changes (pulse rate, breathing, gastric upset, or tremors) are known to occur when a person is anxious. Treatment of anxiety by behavioral and medical management offers effective relief for those who seek it.

Fear is a natural phenomenon of mankind (and animals) that is best treated by behavioral methods. Pills exist for the management of anxiety and depression, but chemical management of fear is unlikely since there is no known antidote that has proved effective in calming the fear response.

Treating Aerophobia: A Rationale.

As a psychologist, I favor an eclectic approach in viewing behavior, that is, I do not subscribe totally to any one school of psychological theory or treatment technique. Instead, I feel free to borrow from the broad array of theories that focus on behavior and that offer suggestions for change. The practice of psychology, like medicine, is both an art and a science.

Graduate training of psychologists is intense in learning the use of psychological tests for making a diagnosis. When disorders are suspected, the clinician determines a treatment plan that will best fit the needs of the client and the skills of the clinician.

Learning theories, especially BEHAVIOR MODIFICATION, provide a practical means for altering human behavior. Clinicians use methods that have stood the test of rigorous research and experimentation. The goal is to achieve a "shaping" of behavior by the use of positive or negative consequences to "reinforce" or "extinguish" a person's responses, namely:

1) Desired behaviors are handily reinforced with rewards. Rewards are more effective than negative actions. Praise is a more positive reinforcer of behavior than reprimand. Gaining self-confidence is a powerful reward.

2) Undesired behaviors may be extinguished (or changed, with difficulty) by withholding rewards or by applying a negative consequence. Fear is a negative consequence; the lessening of fear becomes a positive reinforcer.

Behavior therapy methods focus on the reduction of anxiety by **systematically desensitizing** the person to the feared situation by a controlled, gradual, non-threatening exposure to the anxiety-provoking situation. Unreasonable fears diminish as a result of the "conditioning" processes. We can all recall events when we were once fearful, only to have the fear vanish after a benign, uneventful encounter.

Being rid of fear is a tremendous reward in itself. Desire to overcome a dreaded condition is a strong motivator, and motivation is an important factor in effecting change. Token rewards are effective motivators. For example, a child, fearful of the dark, gains comfort from the parent's assurance of safe being (preferably while in the dark area). But if the child receives a pleasant reward (ice cream) at the time, his fear fades faster. Reward strengthens desired behaviors and counters fear.

A comfortable framework to work within when dealing with aerophobia involves an examination of both the **rational** and **emotional** problems. Since phobias involve an irrational impact on emotion, a focus on the emotional aspects will yield greater initial benefit.

In aerophobia, logical discussion of the safety of air travel must wait until the resultant emotional **feelings** are brought under some measure of control. Recovery is measured when fear diminishes enough to allow a more rational encounter with the once feared situation.

Behavior therapies have proved more effective in treating the phobic disorders than other treatment methods including psychoanalytical psychotherapy. Even Freud concurred in the need for behavioral techniques such as "exposure" for treating phobias when he stated:

"One succeeds only (in overcoming phobias) when one can induce them (the phobic persons) to go about alone and to struggle with their anxiety while they make the attempt (to confront the feared situation)."

This statement belies the notion that Sigmund Freud was not eclectic in his views. In fairness, he honestly saw the utility of techniques other than "couch analysis" alone.

ASSERTIVENESS TRAINING is another means of effecting behavioral change, especially in those who are unable or reluctant to express their feelings openly to others.

Passive or timid persons harbor undue amounts of anxiety when they suppress their thoughts, feelings, and wishes. Learning to express resentment honestly and assertively to others enhances our self-confidence and serves to lower anxieties in interpersonal matters.

Intimidation is devastating to the overly shy and fearful person. A successful businessman stated he viewed the airplane as a "threatening tool of destruction," which intimidated him and disturbed his self-confidence. Assertively, to himself, he challenged his views by seeing the airplane as "just another means of travel" in the same way he regarded a bus, train, or boat. It worked for him.

For those who need to express their concerns more freely, becoming more assertive provides interesting benefits. Honest assertion of feelings toward others often helps to resolve vague conflicts in personal matters. Granted, there is a risk that new conflicts may arise in existing relationships, but skillful assertiveness can enhance self-confidence for the shy and fearful. Timidity takes a back seat while fear subsides. And at times, showing agitation is preferred to being "frozen with fear!"

In addition, COGNITIVE THERAPY is beneficial as the method focuses on restructuring the reasoning and thinking processes that influence our attitudes toward ourselves and others. Distorted perceptions may yield negative emotions. Internal beliefs (cognitions), even when they may be irrational, influence our feelings and actions (behavior).

Similarly, this feedback of feelings affects our thoughts, again providing evidence of an inescapable mind-body involvement.

Positive thinking is a cognitive concept that focuses on the avoidance of negative thoughts and attitudes. In the seminars on aerophobia, I ask each participant to focus on the statement, "I can remain calm and under control in an airplane." All participants then say it aloud as a group, and they are encouraged to say it silently during the relaxation drills.

For many, the rituals learned in the relaxation exercises become welcomed tools and are equally effective in reducing stress in other areas of living.

Group participation offers individuals valuable support for facing up to their irrational concerns. I am impressed by the dramatic effectiveness of "group dynamics" in resolving flying fears, especially when the group participates on an actual flight. The shared feelings and humorous jibes of fatalism make light of the event and the exposure to flight is much less threatening.

What then, are the preferred methods for resolving aerophobia? After many years of observing and working with aerophobics both individually and in group seminars, I believe that treatment of the discomforts can best be managed by a combination of **behavioral** and **cognitive** methods, applied in supportive settings. Research literature confirms the choice of these techniques by concluding:

1) Studies of outcome support the usefulness and efficacy of behavioral procedures in treating ·phobias.

2) Exposure (a behavioral technique) was most effective in 17 of 18 studies.

3) Complete remission of the phobia is rare, but most persons tend to become less phobic and experience only minimal disruption of work and social activities.

4) Medication improved the outcome when phobias were associated with anxiety or panic attacks.

In undergoing psychoanalysis to seek relief from a fear of flying, you should be prepared for a lengthy period spent (tradionally in repose on a couch) unravelling the earliest recollections of sexual arousals, toilet training, sibling rivalry, internal and interpersonal conflicts, and ambivalent (love-hate) feelings toward authority figures, usually (parents.)

Change can be painfully·slow while both therapist and patient attempt to work through the "unearthing" of a panoply of unconscious experiences to gain insight into the causes of an irrational behavior.

How valid is this formulation? Who knows? Moreover, modifying behavior does not rest on the accuracy of "cause," nor on "why" a behavior comes about. Knowing "how" to accomplish a desired change is an effective means of reshaping behavior.

Freud agreed that insight alone will not be sufficient for overcoming a phobic fear. Whatever the therapy technique, it is imperative that the therapist consider the goal of gaining a rational control of emotionally distorted feelings.

If change is to occur, behavioral techniques are more conserving of time and expense for the client, without exploring elusive, deep-seated, experiences that may remain but conjectures at best.

Phobias are fraught with mystery. The sources of fear may never be fully known by either client or therapist. Regardless, lacking insight into the "cause" of a phobia should not impede treatment of any disconcerting behavior. The symptoms of a phobia are treatable, and symptomatic relief is a legitimate and most welcome goal.

A combination of behavioral modification, relaxation training with biofeedback techniques, systematic desensitization, short-term psychotherapy, and hypnotherapy are the treatment styles preferred by most clinicians today.

One research psychiatrist, Dr. K. Roy Mackenzie, supports the more flexible, adaptive (to the individual) form of treatment: using the "best fit" techniques among the broad variety available between brief psychoanalysis and the behavioral treatment methods.

Versatility is the key in selecting the mode of treatment for optimal gain in treating aerophobia. The broad spectrum of behavioral techniques constitutes the program followed in the seminars at KUMC.

Relating Freud's notions of psychosexuality always provides the groups with comedy relief. Tension lessens when a sprinkling of titillating tales is offered. Equating flying with the sex act (with tongue-in-cheek) has offered just such relief, humorously. There is little other utility in explaining behavior by the use (or abuse) of such symbolism.

I prefer to assign the causes of a fear of flying to "unknowns that may or may not become known." Insight may be useful, but it is not crucial to a successful outcome.

A more pragmatic view satisfies my clinical analysis of the fear of flying. Freudian followers might question such flexibility, but for the vast majority of clients in the seminars, it works — and without a couch!

Chapter 4

WHEN FEAR INTERFERES: The Body Defends

The mind and body are more than married, for they
are intimately united; when one suffers,
the other sympathizes.

Lord Chesterfield

What the mind envisions, the body manifests. Our thoughts and emotions are processes that strongly affect our feelings, physically. What we call emotions are products of the activities of our nervous and endocrine (hormonal) systems. Emotions and feelings may be looked on as a "sixth sense" evidence of the **mind-body connection.**

Emotionally, we can be glad or sad or mad. Joy is an emotion. Fear is an emotion; so is anger. The role that emotions play in influencing our physical well-being provides a framework for examining the "anatomy" of fear.

Emotions are universal. For many years anthropologists have conducted extensive studies among various cultures and societies; they have found remarkable similarities in the expression of human emotion. Aborigines display laughter and show grief at the same events that evoke similar reactions in a sophisticated New Yorker.

Moreover, learning and maturation modifies the expression of emotion. For example, a child experiencing delight may laugh aloud, while a more restrained adult will only smile at the same event.

A fear of heights (acrophobia) involves a fear of falling, and both fears are commonly observed in human beings and many terrestrial animals. Newborn infants startle when released from support. Later, development and maturation are necessary to acquire a sensation of heights. This suggests a universal learning process is inherent in man's acquisition of dread. Sorting "nature" from "nurture" is seldom an easy task.

Darwinian researchers attribute these phenomena to man's earlier tree-borne ancestry. Falling asleep had dire meaning to one who dozed off while perched in a tree. Could this early influence have a bearing on today's insomniac who has difficulty in "falling" asleep? Plausible, but we can only speculate.

It is fair to say we all have tendencies to feel uneasy looking down from a great height. Peering down into a canyon is breathtaking for some, but paralyzing for others. Many experience an unexplainable urge to "let go" when feeling the surge of adrenaline that signals their fears, a feeling that subsides only when escape is made to a safe haven, or by refraining from looking down. Escape provides only temporary relief; unfortunately, fear remains as long as avoidance persists.

Fear of high places is overcome in certain activities or occupations where adaptation is required. Mountain climbers, or steelworkers in high-rise construction, adapt well. Exposure is the key to their adjustment. They become more adept as they remain high aloft, thereby gaining confidence. The same holds true for overcoming a fear of flying.

It is my impression that a fear of heights has much less to do with a fear of flying than is popularly thought the case. A true fear of height, such as looking over a cliff, results from a feeling of a lack of visual support or restraint when viewing over a vastness of space. In an airliner cabin, there should be no more physical sensation of height than looking out of a car window, since visual space is similar; it's the thought that disturbs.

I have found it helps to visualize the cabin of large airliners to be much like a hotel or theatre lobby. **Controlled visual imagery** works well for those who learn to use the technique.

Many emotional factors, other than a fear of height and falling, are involved in the formation of flying fears. For example, interpersonal and social factors are frequently involved in aerophobia. Learning these factors is of great help in our program. Revealing some of them serves as a framework for working through the problem by a process of "learning and conditioning."

One example, fear of confinement, which is suggestive of claustrophobia, is more frequently mentioned as a cause of marked physical discomfort than is a fear of high places or of falling.

Whatever his cultural background, man mediates his emotions through activity in his brain and peripheral nervous system. What we say "we feel" is the result of internal chemical actions radiating along nerve and blood vessel pathways.

Extensive animal research by physiologists and psychologists has been directed to specific biochemical changes that result from emotional influences. Observable physical reactions are often predictably similar in man.

33

Acute fear is readily detectable in facial and vocal expressions; the internal responses (blood pressure, heart rate, etc.) are less obvious. Regardless, chronic emotional stresses (sustained fear, anger, depression) can be the source of physical symptoms that are often diagnosed as **psychosomatic disorders** when the physical manifestations stem from an emotional source.

To understand how fears can be reduced, or possibly extinguished, it is necessary to look at the nature of fear and how most fears are learned.

Fear: A Learned Response

Some fears are **instinctive.** By definition, instinctive fears are present at birth, universal to a species, and are not learned. However, psychologists generally consider most specific fears are **learned.**

At birth, we have an inborn capacity for fear. For example, extremes of stimulation will elicit a startle reaction in a newborn baby. Loud noises, temperature extremes, inflicted pain, or radical shifts in posture (as in being dropped) intensify these fears — possibly the earliest expression of emotion.

Excitability is an expression of emotion clearly present at birth. Undoubtedly, there are more inborn reactions that are too subtle to be identified.

With maturity to middle childhood, fear stems from the perception of threatening situations, real or imagined. Fear of the dark or being left alone are common for children from six to ten years of age.

Soon after, social situations that involve peer humiliation or rejection become feared. In adolescence and young adulthood, social situations that threaten self-image and confidence become a source of concern that sets the scene for long-term emotional problems. Most common are the anxiety and phobic disorders that evolve from these early-age experiences.

We can be reasonably certain that no one is born with aerophobia. Infants and small children are delightful air travellers; the aerophobic parent is not.

A child may be innocently attracted to a colorful snake (more so if it rattles), but his joy soon turns to fear when he witnesses a negative parental reaction to the snake. There is evidence that some primates (chimpanzees and monkeys) have an inborn fear of snakes and snake-like objects. Any remnants of such innate fear in man may invalidate this analogy, but then, snake-handling can be learned: a plus for learning!

Fear is easily acquired in infants and children. Unwittingly, adults are excellent teachers of emotional reactions, and learning plays a major role in the acquisition of certain emotions, especially fear.

Consider children at play in an amusement park. For many, the rides are thrilling and hold no threat for them, while a fearful parent may choose to be only an observer. Fun for a child frequently translates to fear for the adult.

Has the adult **learned** to fear the roller coaster that he once rode time and again? When does thrill turn to fear? Why does the tingle turn to terror? Why is one person titillated while another is terrorized by the same event? Mysteries abound in the causes and origins of fear.

What is the role of learning and maturation in this disparity? Maturity should give us the edge in coping with the complexities of life. Why then, do we permit the free spirit of youth to diminish with age? Is it that feelings of security are an innocence that erodes with maturity? It appears so. Insecurities proliferate among those suffering from anxiety and fear. Self-doubt is pervasive!

When fear evolves in later stages of life, a good case is made for the role of learning. Psychologists consider "that which is learned, may be unlearned." **Extinction** is the term used in learning theory to account for the unlearning process.

Fear is learned when we become **sensitized** to an object, event, or situation. Desensitization is the term that describes the process of modification or extinction of an acquired fear. Some measure of exposure is necessary to accomplish any reduction in fear of a sensitized condition. Safe distances from feared situations will offer a feeling of **only** temporary security. Fear ruminates until one confronts the issue in a rational, reassuring, and planned course of involvement with the feared situation.

Fear and anxiety are unpleasant emotions that usually call for the desire to avoid a situation. Thrill, excitement, and joy, are seen as incentives. We are motivated to seek pleasure and to avoid pain, which in philosophy is called hedonism, and man is naturally hedonistic.

Since fear encourages avoidance, avoiding flight only reinforces further avoidance. The dread of flight will persist until corrective action is taken to overcome the impact of those discomforts that are sensed while flying.

A fearful flyer suffers mixed emotions in his state of unnerving inner conflict when he is torn between the desire to "approach" a vacation on a tropical isle and the intense urge to "avoid" the flying necessary to get there. It's an example of the classic **approach-avoidance conflict** that is well-known in psychology.

But fear is not always detrimental; consider being capsized in a canoe. Initial reaction should alert the survival instinct and direct the victim to take corrective action: to stay afloat and summon help. Fear often provides us with a safety net that averts danger.

To lessen the intensity of fear, we must first "listen to our bodies" to sense (feel) the physical reactions. The physical effects of fear should arouse the need to **take control of our reactions if we are unable to control the situation** that triggers the dreaded feelings. Where phobias are involved, it is helpful to realize that **it's not the event, but it is our reaction to the event that is our nemesis!**

Fear As A Stressor

For many, anticipation of fear can be as distressing emotionally as the real encounter. The body, unable to know the difference, reacts similarly whether the fear stems from a vivid imagination or from a real event.

Fear frustrates, irrational fear more so. Frustration often leads to aggression (a psychological axiom) that sets the stage for the "fight or flight" reaction to fear.

Fear also distresses. Animals observed in research show a variety of unusual behavioral and physiological changes that result from stressful, fear-induced reactions.

Prolonged stressful exposure results in lasting physical change as well. Animals subjected to repeated physical stress show evidence of enlarged adrenal glands. Rats exposed to a sustained threat develop inflammation of their arteries. Given sufficient stress, man is as vulnerable to physical disorder as the laboratory animal.

Traditionally, gastric upset and ulceration have been associated with chronic emotional distress, although not all persons react to the same degree. Some specific examples of physical change as a result of emotional stress will illustrate the complexity of the mind-body interaction.

The following bodily signs (and possible symptoms of fear) were reported in a study of 4500 air crewmen while flying combat missions in World War II. They were asked: "During combat missions did you feel...?"

	Often	Sometimes	Total
Pounding heart/ rapid pulse	30%	56%	89%
Muscle tension	0	50	83%
Dryness mouth/ throat	30	50	80%
Nervous perspiration	26	3	79%
Nervous stomach	23	53	76%
Frequent urination	25	40	65%
Trembling	11	53	64%
Weakness or fainting	4	37	41%
Memory problems	5	34	39%
Nausea	5	33	38%
Loss of bladder/ bowel control	1	4	5%

(*Introduction to Psychology 4th Edition, Hilgard/Atkinson*)

These physical symptoms are correlated with the presence of fear as an emotion. It is not difficult to see our thoughts and feelings are antecedent to bodily changes.

The dualistic view of mind-body relations implies the body not only takes heed of our emotions, but our emotions are influenced by conditions in our body. It's an inseparable two-way interaction. In the case of fear and stress, we suffer doubly, both physically and emotionally.

The phobic flyer can tell all about the physical feelings. He becomes hostage to complex feelings of uneasiness and to a sense of impending panic, doom, or even death! It's little wonder that great effort is expended to avoid flying, when gripped with such fear.

The mere thought of flying sets the heart pounding, breathing becomes irregular, hands tremble; faintness is felt and the stomach churns and often burns. These feelings of fear are automatic reactions of the sympathetic nervous system that intensify one's anxiety while forging a tightening chain of physical discomforts.

Consider any fear that doesn't make sense to you or to others, particularly to those close to you. It's a safe bet you have been told, "It's all in your head" and you may even be convinced it is, but does this answer alter the situation or reduce the anxiety you feel? Probably not. Since our bodies bear the brunt of our emotions, let's explore how the body reacts to fear.

Thoughts originate in the frontal portion of the brain. Feelings (emotions) occur in the lower, more primitive, midbrain (limbic system). A perceived threat, imagined or actual, will stimulate the body to initiate its defense reaction. In a matter of milliseconds, the threat alerts the nervous system which stimulates the adrenal glands to unleash a charge of adrenaline into the bloodstream — ready for action in an instant — and the entire process starts with an effortless thought!

The body is now supplied throughout with the stimulative effects of the adrenaline-enriched blood. The heart rate increases, breathing speeds up, and blood begins to pool in the muscles to provide energy for attacking or fleeing. Digestion stops, pupils dilate, and perspiration provides body cooling, while untold other automatic alerting actions take place to make ready the body's defenses.

But what if it's a false alarm? The body can't sort that out. It has to be ready! Once a thought has triggered the **alerting** mechanisms, the body runs its course of **resistance** to whatever real or imagined peril it sensed. This stage of resistance may remain in effect until a state of **exhaustion** is reached.

Often this alarm response is a considerable waste of effort and energy and does little to conserve the body's vital resources. You may have noticed this residual effect after a close call or mishap — the trembling, anxious feeling is slow to dissipate once these physical changes occur.

The foregoing process is a concept of the late Hans Selye, noted Canadian physiologist, who described it as the "General Adaptation Syndrome." Selye viewed three stages of response that are inevitable in the body's attempt to adapt to a given sufficient stress. They are as follows: (1) Alerting, (2) resisting, until (3) exhaustion sets in. When recovery occurs, the body is then in readiness for the next onslaught of stress, and so it goes, ad infinitum!

Stress has many definitions. Disputes abound. Emotional stress may be viewed as the result of a continuing demand for resistance or adaptation, when the stage of exhaustion has set-in. I liken it to the physical concept of **strain.**

The mind-body relation is a constant source of research by physiology, neurology, biochemistry, and the behavioral sciences. The interaction of thought (mind) and feeling (body) we find to be undeniably a two-way process.

The Anatomy of Fear

As described earlier, the physical reactions to fear stem from the involuntary sympathetic nervous system which, when alerted, sets into action the resistances that excite myriad physical signs: shortness of breath, fast-beating or hard-pounding heart, and trembling muscles. These are all normal reactions to fear, and they follow Selye's version of stress adaptation.

Self-induced stress can unwittingly trigger panicky feelings. Often, panic attacks are spontaneous with no known cause for the devastating onset. Anticipation and vigilance can bring on an assault. Specific situations that have precipitated anxiety previously, frequently set the scene for recurrent attacks.

Often, subtly disguised physical conditions are known to play a major role in producing emotional stresses. For example, a physical problem that has been involved in airsickness has been linked to the onset of phobic reactions.

Airsickness is a discomforting experience that is compounded with public embarrassment. Nausea can be caused by either **motion** or **emotion,** or both! Vertigo, in any setting, can be frightening. Social concerns mount with either symptom of nausea or vertigo. Sensitivities overwhelm the sensibilities. It is not difficult to see emotional stress or physical discomfort is magnified when a person is open to public scrutiny.

One researcher now suspects an inner-ear (location of the sense of balance) disturbance as the source of the phobic anxiety many feel while riding in elevators, boats, thrill rides, or airplanes. Bizarre? Not at all. The cause is a complicated interaction of neurological processes that work something like this. Gravitational changes that physically upset the sense of balance and cause nausea or vertigo may well become a source of emotional disturbances. Thrill rides are quick to cause dizziness, gastric upset, and intense fear in those with a low tolerance for physical disorientation.

When an inner-ear problem is diagnosed with symptoms of vertigo or nausea, medication (Meclezine) has proved effective in alleviating the physical symptoms. Moreover, a surprising beneficial side effect has emerged (not all side effects of medicine are detrimental) when anti-vertigo medication is effective in dampening the subtle motion nausea: elevators are more easily tolerated, and airplane travel is less threatening. Apparently, treating the physical upset (in the inner ear) eases the impact of emotional upset!

Explanation of this physical problem is best understood by neurologists, physicians, or physicists, but it is an intriguing notion that medication may have solved more than the vertigo. Anxiety attacks, panic disorders, and phobic reactions also diminished with the medication, which is more evidence of the body-mind interplay.

Another physical disorder related to emotional distress involves the heart. A benign, minor condition diagnosed as a "mitral-valve prolapse" (MVP) is suspected of bringing on panic attacks. MVP is a mechanical abnormality found mostly in females, and overall, in nearly 20 percent of otherwise healthy persons. It's only speculation, but MVP could account for more women than men being vulnerable to anxiety and panic disorders. Although, some one-third of those having panic attacks do reveal evidence of MVP problems, it is still uncertain whether MVP is a "cause" or a "symptom" of intense anxiety. MVP disorders may go undetected and be silent contributors to the onset of panic attacks!

Though the relation of MVP to panic disorder is unclear, approximately ten percent of clients attending the aerophobia seminars (12 women and 4 men) were previously diagnosed as having heart murmurs or MVP conditions. They felt an unusual sense of relief when their fear and discomfort with flying might be explained by a non-threatening physical condition. Learning this seemed to solve the mystery of their miseries, and they soon became more confident in being able to fly. "Cure" is ofttimes capricious!

The Chemistry of Fear

Disruption of body chemistry is critical, though subtle, in the production of emotional upset. The delicate balance of internal chemical states has strong influence on emotions and feelings. Awareness of this connection helps clarify the role biochemical factors play in emotional disturbances, especially anxiety.

Many chemical agents are known to affect our feelings and behavior. Caffeine stimulates, alcohol alters moods, nicotine constricts blood vessels, while aspirin eases blood flow and soothes pain. Bouts of anxiety often occur mysteriously as a result of silent, internal chemical change.

Body-chemistry is easily upset with oxygen imbalance. Lack of oxygen (hypoxia) is critical to life. Overbreathing (hyperventilation) results in lightheadedness or dizziness that excites the person to gasp for more air, which further upsets oxygen balance by depleting carbon dioxide in the bloodstream. A "catch-22" situation results with further oxygen imbalance. The quick cure for hyperventilation is the "paper bag trick." Breathing deeply into a paper bag allows the victim to rebreathe his own carbon dioxide correcting the chemical imbalance. A simpler means of regaining proper oxygen balance is **calming and slowing the breathing cycle.** It's quite effective and requires no equipment, not even a paper bag!

Ongoing studies in biochemistry and pharmacology emphasize research in the biological processes to discover agents that will correct chemical imbalances in the body.

In addition to the endocrine glands, the human brain is a virtual apothecary, producing chemical compounds rivaling the most modern pharmaceutical manufacturer. The brain manufactures some compounds routinely, and produces other chemical agents when needed, as in times of stress.

At this writing, scientists have discovered and isolated many new compounds (more than 30) in brain studies. It will take years to know their full influence on man's mental, emotional, and physical states.

These natural chemical agents provide a variety of influences. Some are known to act as stimulants that energize activity, while others serve as sedatives yielding a state of drowsy calmness. Even a sense of euphoria derives from some internally produced elements that lift the spirits. All these agents are capable of creating a variety of effects on mood as well as on physical function.

These internal body substances are identified as hormones and enzymes or as more complex electrochemical agents. Some have a profound influence on feeling, thinking, and behaving. For example, depression is often the result of an internal chemical imbalance which psychiatrists treat with counteracting, anti-depressant medication.

One such form of body product which the brain manufactures emulates a pure form of morphine. It is called an endorphin, and its effects offer an "analgesic" feeling of extreme well-being.

Modern pharmacology has made great strides. Tranquilizers take the edge off anxiety and tension, and sometimes, fear. Sedatives serve as hypnotics that induce sleep. Stimulants energize when energies ebb. Antidepressants lift the grey veil of depression.

Other agents (neuroleptics) correct imbalances in mental functioning by blocking psychotic thought or activity.

As yet, an internal substance that lessens fear has not been isolated. Sad to say, fear as a primary target remains without any known biochemical antidote.

Research continues at a mind-boggling pace, but still much suffering persists. We are left with the necessity of adapting to stress using mostly our own resources and intellects. We can only hope to achieve a stability between the whimsical internal processes and our external environs.

Under stress, the complex body-chemistry balances are often easily disrupted. In the healthy person, intricate internal mechanisms in the brain and nervous system attempt to maintain watch over and to regulate those forces which tend to upset the body's equilibrium, thus acting as a "governor" of sorts.

Homeostasis: The Body's Governor of Stress

Homeostasis refers to the body's built-in tendency to maintain internal stability by adjusting to conditions that otherwise may threaten one's health.

Dr. Walter B. Cannon, a famed Harvard physiologist, viewed homeostasis as a protective device for maintaining the equilibrium of bodily processes when stress is encountered.

Cannon saw the major benefit of homeostasis in "liberating the nervous system from the necessity of paying routine attention to the management of the details of bare existence. Without homeostatic devices we should be in constant danger of disaster, unless we were always on the alert to correct voluntarily what normally is corrected automatically.'' A miraculous process.

Adaptation and maintenance of a stabilized state is upset when stress sounds an alerting signal, and as described earlier (in this chapter,) Hans Selye's ''game plan for adapting'' comes into play. Internal forces mobilize automatically to resist and defend against whatever changes occur in the body's physical and chemical balances. Externally (behaviorally), man resorts to attacking (fight) or avoiding (take flight) the stressful situation.

The ''fight or flight'' phenomenon implies two choices: attack or flee! Actually, there's a third option. It is immobility or a non-response. The opossum uses this mode of defense astutely at times, appearing dead or frozen-like to his enemy.

Whatever the choice, reaction to fear presents a stressful dilemma. When fight, flight or freeze are not acceptable, an **avoidance conflict** intensifies the stress reaction and creates a vulnerable condition.

Emotional and internal physical stress reactions result from such encounters. Stress-related illnesses produce physical symptoms, but not always physical change. The circulatory and digestive systems are the regions most vulnerable to emotional stress, as evidenced in the study of WW II combat fliers mentioned earlier.

In the ''fight-or-flight'' dilemma, what you may not know is your **autonomic** nervous system (ANS) has taken its battle station for your defense in resisting the upset caused by a stressful situation.

The autonomic nerves act on the muscle of the heart and glands in the body, which are not normally under voluntary control. The ANS portion of the body serves to make those adjustments which are necessary to maintain a physiological equilibrium, whether the stress is physical, mental, or emotional.

Adaptation relies largely on the process of homeostasis, that is, the automatic adjustments within our nervous and endocrine systems that maintain a healthy physical state — with little or no effort on our part when all goes well.

Stress ''overload'' may be viewed as **a continuance of a stressful stimulation after exhaustion has occurred.** With excessive or continued stress, the adaptive process suffers.

Adaptation is necessary to emotional as well as physical forces of stress. We are well aware of physical fatigue, but emotional exhaustion is often disguised until a crisis occurs, which is often described as an "emotional (or nervous) breakdown."

Emotional upset, such as that caused by intense fear, challenges the adaptive processes of homeostasis. A general uneasiness over any period may produce vague bodily symptoms as reactions.

In mild fear, the symptoms of stress are subtle and tolerable. Physical change is negligible.

Moderate levels of fear produce more notable physical symptoms such as tremors, shortness of breath, a hollow feeling in the stomach, a clammy chill, or cold sweat.

Extreme levels of fear excite the pulse and cause a pounding of the heart that is felt throughout the body. Lasting physical changes are more likely.

The mind-body connection is undeniable. But what can we do to lessen its reactions to stress? We know much more than the cave man knew, but unfortunately we have also acquired many more fears than those he confronted.

Little has changed since the evolution of the cave man to modern man, other than a greater mastery of his external environment. Modern man continues to react internally in a similar primitive fashion in spite of vast cultural changes. His society has advanced through the elaboration of communication and other technologies. Greater emphasis on reasoning and intellectual functioning has evolved, but there is little change in his emotional responses.

Learning is his best weapon for improving his adaptation to the world as it is today. Control of the emotions is largely an intellectual (cognitive) process and is therefore learnable and amenable to change.

Cave man reactions in the jet age are not only untimely, but they are the major source of problems in coping with the complexities of modern living. The cave man may have sensed a fear of heights or falling and even a fear of flying predators, but never a fear of flying!

Our fears too often interfere with our quest for quality in our living. Elan Vital — the good life — does not come easily, but not to despair; gaining control of our emotions is a reality which, once learned, can bring a "harmony in living" that has evaded all those whose lives are fraught with fear. The following chapter will provide some keys for escaping to a new-found freedom from fear, especially, an unreasonable fear of flying.

Chapter 5

PROFILES OF AEROPHOBIA

The causes of phobias in general and aerophobia in particular are often unknown. Most researchers and clinicians acknowledge this gap in understanding. As a result, practitioners have to settle for treating the symptoms, and they do so effectively because the sources remain a mystery.

For physicians, symptoms serve as clues for diagnosis and treatment. They can look for observable signs in a patient. Is there fever, rash, fracture, irregularity of blood pressure?

In the search for clues to mental and emotional problems, psychologists are left with only overt behavior for objective signs in making their diagnoses. Subjectively, symptoms are often denied or disguised until the client reveals his feelings and thoughts to a clinician. Much must be inferred. Medicine and psychology demand a blend of both "art **and** science" in their practices.

Objective confirmation does not come easily, therefore, the underlying causes of mental and emotional disorders are often only speculative at best.

Occasionally the source of a phobia is known. For example, a person badly frightened by a snake may develop a morbid dread of reptiles, whereas another person also frightened by a snake might never admit to his undue fear or recover from the episode with no aftereffects at all. Why does a traumatic experience grow into a phobia in one person and not in another? No one is sure.

Regardless, treatment of the symptoms can be initiated effectively without knowing the complete picture of the underlying cause or causes. Relief, if not cure, is quite possible and is always welcomed.

From the nearly 200 aerophobics I have studied so far, four characteristic patterns of behavior have surfaced which dominate the aerophobics' makeup personality and thus his style of living. Such traits may be regarded as predisposing factors or "weak spots" in their makeup toward living, and they are seen as determinants of a susceptibility to being phobic, particularly aerophobic. These four factors involve: generalized anxiety, problems of personal control, claustrophobia, and separation anxiety. Further description of these behavioral patterns will help in identifying those traits that are central to a fear of flying.

1) **GENERALIZED ANXIETY** involves a variety of attitudes and personality traits such as perfectionism, obsessive thoughts, persistent anxiety, indecisiveness, avoidance, procrastination, apprehensive expectations, chronic doubting (of self and others), negativeness, excessive vigilance, irritability, and impatience.

Physical manifestations of generalized anxiety are often observed as nervousness, body tension, heart-pounding, dry mouth, clammy hands, dizziness, lump in throat, breathing irregularity, gastric upset, and numerous other autonomic (sympathetic) nervous system signs.

Emotional adjustment is extremely difficult for those with such profuse anxiety.

2) **CONTROL PROBLEMS.** Excessive control concerns involve a fear of **losing self-control** , or a disturbing uneasiness when **others are in control** of given situations (a distinct difference).

Strong feelings of social embarassment threaten those who fear they may lose self-control in a public situation. Passivity, timidity, insecurity, and strong **dependency** needs mark many who suffer unduly in anticipation of a failure to cope with a situation. They are trusting of others, but self-doubt burdens them.

Those with a fear of ''not being in control'' of their destinies often lack trust in others. Feelings of security rest on their own **self-reliance** and **independence.** When one is forced to depend on others, an uneasy sense of helplessness may frustrate, anger, depress, or frighten. For them, life is intense.

3) **CLAUSTROPHOBIA.** Signs of physical reactions that produce a feeling of extreme discomfort and fear when one is confined in close places; feelings of suffocation, or constricted movement are classic symptoms of claustrophobia.

Evidence of confinement problems (other than when flying) confirms the role of claustrophobia that adds to an aerophobic's uneasiness and fears. For example, many aerophobics have difficulty tolerating elevators and tunnels. Thoughts of being trapped will bring on panicky feelings and a resultant need for escape. Many behavioral researchers view claustrophobia as a central factor involved in all phobic disorders.

4) **SEPARATION ANXIETY.** Inappropriately strong feelings of apprehension occur in some persons when they are away from home or are separated from loved ones. In many, the earliest evidence appears during childhood in the form of school phobia. Even temporary separation can cause problems of adjustment in adulthood, although the mature are often more adept at disguise (even to self) than are children.

These four patterns of behavior and personality traits (general anxiety, control problems, claustrophobia, and separation anxiety) have emerged as central features among those who have participated in the aerophobia seminars at KUMC.

These personality patterns are not mutually exclusive. Often two or more affect aerophobics, but one trait usually dominates. Many persons reveal a high state of self-concern and admit to being overly sensitive in social situations other than flying. Public scrutiny makes them feel uneasy, and social embarrassment is unbearable, therefore a diagnosis of "social phobia" best describes the majority of those attending the seminars.

Many have a near-total lack of insight into their fears, but they soon discover more plausible reasons for their psychic pain as the seminar unfolds. This new insight helps, but results of the seminar indicate that such enlightenment is not sufficient in itself. Change in behavior, habit, and attitude is needed to alter their irrational reactions to flying.

A further description of these personality patterns, habits, and attitudes will more clearly define the role they play in the formation of anxiety and emotional stresses evidenced among those suffering a fear of flying.

Personality Factors in Generalized Anxiety

Personality refers to the characteristic way in which a person thinks, feels, and behaves — an ingrained pattern of behavior that each person reveals (consciously or unconsciously) that determines his style of living and the manner in which he adapts to his environment.

Personality traits are judged to be disordered when they impair social or emotional functioning or cause moderate amounts of subjective distress or anxiety.

Obsessive-compulsive neurosis is a dominant factor in the phobic disorders. Obsessions are inescapable thoughts. Compulsions are driven acts.

Frequently, **obsessive** thoughts are mingled with compulsive behaviors although they are separate symptoms. Obsessional ruminations are difficult to resist even when they are recognized as irrational and meaningless thoughts that torment, but avoidance is difficult if not impossible.

Commonly, obsessions among phobic individuals involve traumatic images of a fearful situation. Plane crash tragedies become fixations for aerophobics. The inability to escape such painful thoughts is as baffling as is the logic in attempting to account for masochistic behaviors, and any explanation for self-inflicted pain or torment is fraught with speculation.

For **compulsive** individuals, disorder disturbs; orderliness calms. They are distressed if a compelling urge to perform an act is thwarted. For example, straightening a picture in a public area is suggestive of a "driven" act by one who is inclined to be compulsively perfectionistic. Coy grins by many in the seminar confirm that the urge to straighten pictures was prevalent among them. This example of compulsiveness provides a breakthrough of insight, which for many appears to account for their neurotic uneasiness in other situations beyond their being aerophobic.

Few persons offer rebuttals to protest the implication that such an insignificant sampling of behavior would be suggestive of a neurosis. Most will readily admit their fear of flying is neurotic, but their urge to adjust a picture in disarray is utterly absurd. Or is it?

A desire for orderliness and timeliness is virtuous, but a tendency to agonize over trivial inconveniences is suggestive of being overly rigid in adapting to change. A flight delay, unplanned occurrences, slow food service, or unusual happenings during flight are upsetting. Irritability surfaces for the slightest reason. A loss of luggage is traumatizing, but travel by any mode is subject to unexpected occurrences, and air travel certainly has its share of unusual happenings for those apprehensive of flying.

For psychiatrists and psychologists, neurotic obsessive- compulsive traits are quite difficult to modify. Recent drug research indicates that anti-depressant medication is sometimes effective in lessening obsessional tendencies in neurotically disturbed individuals, but relief, medically or behaviorally, is apparently elusive for many.

To encourage self-examination regarding obsessive-compulsive tendencies, consider the following: It is customary to lock the house when we leave home. Feeling an urge to return to double-check, is not unusual, although if after rechecking, uneasiness and doubting thoughts persist, we are then doubly burdened with obsessional problems.

Small wonder leaving home for any extended time creates considerable anxiety for those who suffer the torment of self-induced obsessive-compulsive tendencies. It is comforting to learn these secret feelings are shared by others and are understandably related to their phobic behaviors.

Typically, many seminar participants are quick to admit compulsiveness has been a problem for them most of their lives. Learning to "shrug your shoulders" at trivial details certainly helps many. Being more flexible in living is effective therapy for the overly rigid and those demanding of perfection from self — and others!

The label "chronic doubter" best describes those who tend to be negatively apprehensive. They consistently anticipate events from a worst possible scenario viewpoint. Risk-taking is frightening. Fear of failure is pervasive. Indecision and procrastination in the simplest tasks lead to chronic anxiety.

Studies of personality factors as they relate to phobic anxiety are limited, but we know that chronic anxiety tends to run in families. For example, studies have revealed that mothers (more than fathers) of anxiety-prone individuals had clinical histories of anxiety disorders. Genetic influence is always difficult to rule out since environment plays a role in chronic anxiety, and disturbances in childhood experiences may persist into adulthood. Gaining awareness of such "hangups" sets the stage for more rational, less emotional attitudes toward their phobic concerns.

Most traits contributing to generalized anxiety emerge in adolescence or early adulthood and are not easily coaxed away. Persons sufficiently motivated have made dramatic gains by modifying those attitudes that have contributed to their problems in living and which have generalized to their fear of air travel! But then, changing attitudes is not done without great travail.

Control Problems

As mentioned, there are two manifestations of fear in this category:
1) Fear of losing self-control often results from anticipating a "panic attack" or becoming unable to control one's emotional reactions. Panic disorders involve discrete periods of apprehension or fear that produce recurrent and reverberating bouts of acute anxiety. Social embarrassment becomes an obsession. Being alone in a crowd and away from home can threaten.

2) Fear of not being in control of one's destiny is unbearable to many. Deferring control to others is painful. This is the "backseat driver's syndrome," which readily describes those individuals who prefer or insist on driving. They are reluctantly uneasy being under another's control in many situations. This concern may appear to be more prevalent among men, although women suffer similarly when they are aggressively inclined and are less passive.

Both problems of control are prevalent in more than half of those attending the seminars. **Passivity** dominates those who fear losing self-control. Those who are ill-at-ease when not in control of a situation tend to be more **aggressively** oriented.

There is a distinct difference in the source of concern and the resulting behavior manifest by these two groups.

More than a third of the seminar participants express a fear of losing self-control. They give vivid accounts of times when strange feelings overcome them with no apparent cause, which describes the nature of an anxiety attack. At such times they are convinced they might "die on the spot." After experiencing these bizarre feelings, they become more apprehensive and anticipate further attacks with some regularity. Feeling so hopelessly fragile, they insist that flying would surely precipitate such an attack, hence they are left with avoidance as their only choice!

Feeling threatened away from home is a major symptom of agoraphobia. A diagnosis of agoraphobia (which required treatment) had been made in some eight percent of those attending the seminars, many of them referred from the Agoraphobia Clinic at KUMC. I viewed this as an encouraging sign of recovery when one who is too fearful to venture from home seeks relief from a fear of flying — for more distant journeys! I'm pleased to report they did well, much credit for which must be given their treatment prior to attending the aerophobia seminars.

On the other hand, for many of us there is a driving need to be in control of our destinies. Leading is preferred; being led is disturbing. Having to defer control to another violates the need for self-sufficiency, which is troublesome to bear for those who treasure their independence.

An intense fear of not being in control is as great a problem as a fear of losing self-control, but it is more frustrating for the clinician because of the accompanying lack of trust in others. It is difficult to win the client's confidence and overcome his dubious attitude toward others.

Flying a jet transport or performing major surgery requires skills that few possess. During flight or surgery, passengers or patients must have confidence, faith, and trust in those "in control" of their destinies.

For those who are dubious about trusting others, flight is out of the question and elective surgery is unthinkable. When either air travel or surgery is deemed necessary, the anguish is unbearable. In fairness, it should be said there are some skilled pilots who are reluctant to fly as passengers while some surgeons will resist any form of elective surgery for themselves. It is not so much they distrust their peers, but in their autocratic way, they prefer to be in command!

The need for being in control of outcomes is shared by many of us regardless of the task or situation, but perhaps, those who are less rigid "riding in a backseat" suffer less by being more adaptive.

Unmasking the underlying factors that accompany a strong need to control others is challenging. Their doubts of others is pervasive; at times, self-doubts are concealed by overt criticism and becoming irritable with the incompetence of others. They are often impatiently pressed for time; standing in lines demeans; gaining favored attention calms. Forced into the passive roles of passengers, their irritations are intensified when they are by nature hard-driving, demanding, efficiency-oriented, and aggressively assertive individuals. Anger often masks their anxieties. Underlying depressions are frequently disguised by their displays of agitation.

Aggravations mount when they are forced to adhere to someone else's schedule of activities as often occurs in air travel. In public, they are critically observant and vigilant of the performances and slightest miscues of others.

Yes, there is a marked distinction between the passivity of those fearing loss of self-control and those aggresively oriented who suffer when they are not in command of others.

Some personality theorists have described individuals as either "internalizers" or "externalizers" in terms of how they see the locus of control in the world.

Those with an internal orientation assume personal control of their fates; to them, fatalism is unacceptable. By contrast, externalizers see events in life occurring by chance, fate, or other factors not under their control. They are willing to accept their fate rests in others.

Many studies on the "locus of control" describe the distinction between these two traits:

1) **Internals** are achievement-oriented, independent, resistant to influence, successful in their undertakings, severe in judging the actions of others, and prefer tasks that require their own skills.

2) **Externals** are more passive, dependent, timid, and uncertain about their personal skills in performing complex tasks. Social factors are also seen as determinants involved with minorities and lower socioeconomic classes usually being more acceptant of others in control. Surveys seem to confirm that most internals are males, while most externals are females.

These traits are not easily altered, even when the individuals have insight into their problems. Greater effort and motivation are needed to overcome the rigid entrenchment of both traits of passiveness or aggressiveness.

In matters of emotional adjustment, flexibility is necessary; rigidity is self-defeating and will only perpetuate the traits. Confidence and trust in self or others is not easy to come by if doubt and insecurity are too deeply embedded.

Unhealthy attitudes most often contribute to emotional problems. Unfortunately, the attitudes in question are difficult to change. The behavioral sciences are not blessed with a "magic pill" to treat pathologic attitudes as physicians are in treating infections with antibiotics. Industrial strength amounts of reasoning, insight, and motivation are required to effectively change our attitudes about ourselves or others.

Claustrophobia: Don't Fence Me In

Some theorists see claustrophobia as central to all phobic disorders. Uneasiness when confined — whether by space or time — often causes intense physical reactions in those suffering from claustrophobia.

Claustrophobics are frequently uncomfortable in elevators or tunnels, or feeling entombed-like in any vehicle (submarines and airplanes are most notable). Some are even uncomfortable in barber chairs (unbelievable?); more suffer in dentists' chairs (believable!). Mysteries abound when an attempt is made to account for the panic reactions of claustrophobics.

Undoubtedly, feelings of "being trapped" and unable to escape at will are central to the intense pangs of fear that overwhelm those who suffer from claustrophobia.

Through personal experience, I can attest claustrophobia is a nuisance at best and a devastation at worst. At the risk of exposing a personal frailty (pilots should be models of emotional durability), I have openly admitted (in the seminars) that claustrophobia was a problem for me whenever my normal breathing was obstructed. Here's an early experience.

It became necessary for airline pilots to wear a full-face smoke mask (oral-nasal type) during instrument flight examinations, simulating a smoke-filled cockpit.

My first test of this procedure came while being observed in a four-engine Constellation, with a TWA check pilot and an FAA examiner observing the drill. I recall it vividly — even some 30 years later!

On first donning the mask, I became startled as I felt my quickened pulse vibrate through my body into my arms and hands. The tremors subsided only when I gripped the control wheel and throttles harder — and harder. The reaction was an unsettling surprise to me.

My immediate response was hardly conducive to passing a flight check. Reflexively, I wanted to rip off the choking mask, but a quick survey of the problem called for a more rational course; keep cool; demonstrate full-control! To do so, I determined that first I had to regulate my breathing. Rationally I knew there was ample oxygen in the mask chamber, but emotionally I was in doubt!

I diverted my attention to the instruments. Breathing became more relaxed. I checked the airspeed and power settings. This was no time to panic, especially not for a command pilot.

I gained reassurance from an internal self-directed monologue much like a coach's half-time pep talk in a big game. The only choice was to "tough out" the situation. It worked. A calm set in as I regained control of the panic-induced physical reactions.

Soon, tension built again. I devised a strategy: I'd ask a question of the check pilot, allowing me to lift the mask for the briefest moment, which I did (the question was irrelevant I'm sure). This ploy literally gave me a breather with further relaxation before I had to re-position the mask.

By this control plan, however crude, I managed to contain the jolt of adrenaline that charged throughout my body. The approach and landing were uneventful, and I passed the flight exam: but more important, the experience offered a needed challenge for change.

Neither the check pilot nor the FAA inspector suspected the burst of anguish I felt, but I was acutely aware of the need for desensitizing such a classic claustrophobic reaction.

After that episode I set up a routine procedure of donning the mask before each flight. By spending a few extra minutes regulating the race-of-nerves reaction, I managed to subdue the phobic feeling — a dramatic example of **systematic desensitization.** Hatha Yoga emphasizes disciplined breath control to restore vital energy and calm to the body. I can heartily validate the calming effectiveness by regulated breathing.

Oddly enough, the close quarters of cockpits never bothered me while logging over 28 thousand hours of flying time in them. Learning to play the game with the smoke mask solved the breathing problem and claustrophobia was no longer a problem for me in airline operations. In fact, each time the mask was tested, the oxygen came as a refreshing treat!

Rational control of the emotions is more likely and human frailties are more easily managed when a person is relaxed and free of tension. It's as simple as that — and breath control is the key to relaxation and tension reduction! (More on this in Chapter 7.)

Nevertheless, in a later and somewhat different situation, I encountered a recurrence of claustrophobia.

My brother, George, an Air Force fighter pilot, was testing F-102 and F-106 jet fighters in the late 1950s at Edwards Air Force Base in California. (Yes, he served with Chuck Yeager in the jet-testing program at the time.)

George arranged a flight for me in the F-102 so that he could demonstrate the performance of a military jet fighter to his "kid brother, truck-driver airline pilot."

I received a thorough briefing on the delta-wing fighter and was outfitted with the necessary flight suit and helmet. I churned with excitement and anticipated a "thrill of a lifetime" with nary a sign of apprehension in the ready room.

After starting up and while taxiing out, George closed the cockpit hatch and instructed me to secure the face mask on my helmet for the takeoff. As I closed the visor-like device over my face — it happened — again! A sharp burst of adrenaline, a racing pulse, and a feeling of suffocation swept over me — shades of the earlier encounter with oxygen masks!

Again, consciously, I was at once aware of the need to regain control of the reflexive feelings of anxiety. (George never suspected my discomfort.) By this time, I recalled the earlier conditioning, and by controlled, calm breathing, I was able to dispel the agony. By concentrating on the task at hand, I soon recovered and controlled any further physical or emotional ravaging. For an instant, a past dread had surfaced but it was managed by a learned, conscious effort; another credit to controlled breathing.

The thrill of the flight defies description even now. I became convinced such flying demanded the "right stuff" in high doses!

My point in describing this occurrence is to emphasize the "likelihood of relapse" from a once-desensitized state. Over time, and in different situations, sensitivities may recur that demand readaptive effort; an important point to know and remember. Also, it was easier to gain control the second time around.

Relapse is often a part of the course or outcome of many disorders — physically, behaviorally or psychologically — but it should not be considered as failure. A setback is but a hesitation in progress! Regroup and recover is the course to pursue.

The essence of this episode is once having lessened a claustrophobic reaction in the earlier airline situation with the oxygen mask, I was aided later in adjusting to a similar phobic reaction while flying in a military aircraft.

Likewise, varying conditions may yield subtle similarities in adapting to stressful situations. Many clients experience a recurrence of discomfort in their adjustments to subsequent flights and improvement may vary. With planned effort, **despair subsides as confidence and perseverance develop.**

Both rational self-assurance and systematic desensitization should be sufficient to lessen the reactions of claustrophobia. I can verify — it does work!

Separation Anxiety

For some individuals, parting from loved ones causes an emotional dread. Infants and older children often become apprehensive when separated from their mothers or when they are approached by strangers. Baby sitters know this reaction well.

Kindergarten teachers identify such behavior as "school phobia." On occasion, a mother may remain in the classroom with her child for the first few days of school. With proper management by the parent and teacher, the child will gradually adjust to the school environment. An emotional weaning results as the fear of being abandoned gives way to reassurance and desensitization.

Older children frequently suffer "homesickness" when away at summer camp. Many parents experience anxiety when they leave their children for even short periods. Spouses, too, suffer anxieties when temporarily separated from their mates, and divorce produces intense separation anxiety for one or both partners.

Remnants of separation anxiety can re-emerge regressively later in life. Separation from significant others (loved ones or companions) or from comfortable surroundings are known to awaken earlier feelings of insecurity when in unfamiliar situations. Adults who prefer sedentary, home-body ways of living are vulnerable to anxieties when separated from home and family.

Emotional attachments to persons, places, or objects lie dormant until a sense of loss erupts. One woman in the seminar admitted her nervous uneasiness just watching her personal luggage disappear on a baggage conveyor after checking it for a flight. Obviously, strong dependency needs and intense self-doubts are involved in such a reaction.

Feelings of dependency and insecurity are not the only issues involved. Freud spoke of the "loss of love object" as releasing a multitude of neurotic, pent-up feelings. Even temporary parting may simulate such a loss to those suffering the irrational effects of separation anxiety.

One would expect separation anxiety to be a greater problem for women, given their tendencies for strong maternalistic urgings, but men also, are vulnerable for feeling temporary losses in being separated from their home environs. A case in point.

Charles was an administrator for a large corporation. A recent promotion required air travel on a regular basis, but he held an intense fear of flying. His advancement brought mixed emotions and inner conflict. For relief, he enrolled in the seminar.

Asked to describe his problem, Charles confined his concerns and reactions to flying in terms of physical discomfort and unexplainable anxiety. Why? He had never suffered a trauma while flying. His reaction was a mystery which added to his misery. In the seminar, he listened intently and was especially intrigued with the series of relaxation exercises that yielded a profound calming that he had never known.

Three weeks after the seminar Charles called me. There was a note of triumph in his voice: "Walt, my problem **was** separation anxiety!" He was jubilant with his discovery. Charles went on describing his fascination with the rationale in the seminar that explained the relationship between fear and tension, and the methods of relaxation that offered a possible curative effect. He was determined to see if these techniques would work for him. Obviously, he was an avid student.

Charles anticipated his next flight with more curiosity than anxious doubt. He boarded the flight eagerly with his plan well in mind to manage his tension through relaxation. Following the seminar instructions, he timed the takeoff, and once aloft, he distracted himself with reading and the refreshments that were offered. It worked! The flight held no threat for him. He arrived for his business affairs feeling refreshed and overjoyed with his victory over fear! He even grew eager for the return trip — to home, wife, and children — and that eagerness provided an important clue to his discomfort. In analyzing what had taken place, Charles recalled the trip leaving home was always more disturbing than the trip returning. In fact, returning flights were less threatening; the embraces with loved ones at the airport signalled the end of his separation; his anxiety was minimal, if any.

His dilemma explained, Charles now manages his homesickness by anticipating and visualizing his return trip, so now, leaving home is much less stressful than before. In this case, insight proved invaluable for Charles. His promotion is no longer the bittersweet dilemma it had been. He treasures his newly-found freedom and actually looks forward to flying, joyfully!

Generalized anxiety, concern over loss of control, claustrophobia, and separation anxiety are seen as major contributing factors to the symptoms of aerophobia. There may be other issues that are involved in a phobic feeling toward flying, but these four categories best describe our clients in the clinical seminars at KUMC.

All these traits are susceptible to change and the prognosis is favorable for overcoming the fear of flying for those so motivated to explore the methods that may provide adaptive relief.

Nevertheless, for some, the task may prove too challenging. Continued avoidance will only deprive them further of the many pleasures of flight that can be shared with friends and families. Moreover, I regret that many will miss career opportunities that are crucial to their future successes.

For those able to overcome their irrational fears, the rewards are well worth the effort. The choice is theirs — to remain fearful or to gain freedom — which should dictate only one rational decision, but doubt remains a forceful factor in their decision making. And chronic doubting is an attitude that is firmly cloaked in a toughened armor coating — too tough to break out of for many — especially when change threatens. I have wondered if a ''fear of success'' can be part of the problem, but further speculation only confuses rather than clarifies the issues.

Chapter 6

CASE STUDIES: Successes and Failures

During the past twenty years as a psychologist, I have encountered a wide assortment of individuals — children, adolescents, parents, professionals, executives, alcoholics, drug abusers, psychopaths, sociopaths — most clearly neurotic, and some overtly psychotic.

Now, with aerophobics, I do not consider my role as being their psychotherapist. Rather, the relationship is that of a flight instructor whose goal is to assure his students that they can adapt to flying without undue fear — and it works for an encouraging majority — but not without some occasional failures, on my part or theirs.

Here is a sampling of cases that represent a cross-section of those who have attended the aerophobia seminars at KUMC. Feel free to determine who should be accorded with their success or failure, in the outcomes: the instructor, the student, or both. Obviously, I am not using their real names.

JANE: Fear of Not Being in Control

Jane was planning a business trip from Kansas City to St. Louis. Flight time is only one short hour.

The day was dreary, drizzling. Flying in inclement weather always disturbed Jane. As she lingered in the airport terminal, pondering, Jane eyed the parking lot where her car meant escape to the safety of home. She paused and opted first to make a phone call to my office.

Jane had completed the aerophobia seminar the previous week. We had discussed weather and jet flying in a positive and optimistic tone, and she seemed convinced at the time.

When I took her call, Jane was breathless, as though she had dashed to the phone. She described her dilemma with a frantic, trembling tone in her voice as she asked for my evaluation of the weather conditions.

I countered her dubious tone assuredly with "It's a piece of cake; there shouldn't be a bump; nothing but smooth, saturated tropical air mass; good cloud ceiling and visibility. The weather in St. Louis should be much clearer than it is in Kansas City!"

Pilots habitually keep abreast of the weather, and the **Today Show,** which I had watched that morning, was my source of weather forecasting. Somehow, my remarks did not comfort her. Her anguish grew.

Despite my encouragement, a compelling force within Jane left her in doubt, and she was torn with indecision. Sensing her concern, I asked her to take the "six second break," and rehearse the "smile, breathe, relax" procedure she had learned in the class. It worked. By now, her voice calmed, reflecting more composure.

I continued chatting with her and urged her to focus on calming her thoughts saying, "Now, smile, breathe in, and relax!" For further distraction, I suggested she return to the gate area and ask to talk with the Captain of the flight, if possible, and to explain her concerns to him. (I was confident in the effectiveness of an airline pilot's skill in reassuring her.) Sounding much relieved, she agreed. I awaited a further call that never came.

Later on, I checked with her husband, and he confirmed that she had followed my advice. The airline Captain was reassuring, so she left on the flight and all went well. But then, the aftermath was disappointing.

Jane had conducted her business in St. Louis and on the following day when it was time for her return flight, the weather was once again dreary, drizzly, and ominous. She gave no thought to a call to me, or to contact the pilot at the airport. Jane took the train! She had reverted to **escape** and **avoidance** as her solution.

Her husband met the train and they drove home enjoying Kansas City's weather which turned out to be ideal for flying.

In assessing Jane's aerophobia, I saw the prominent feature as her rigid need for being in control — an authoritarian trait, which befits the business executrix that she is.

Jane has little fear of losing self-control, a problem noted in the more passive personalities, and vastly different from her aggressive need to control her own destinies. Internal strength is her forte; doubt and mistrust of others is her Achilles' heel.

Jane deceptively assigned her concerns to the inclement weather. In reality, she expressed an intense fear of "crashing and dying" when others were in control of her fate.

She had gained confidence by talking with the pilot; she admired his "command authority" and felt that she could trust him with control of her life once she had met him, even though briefly. This attitude signalled Jane's lack of "blind trust" in others until she was able to know them on a more personal level. Doubt diminished with familiarity when she was favorably impressed.

Even when driving, Jane was more at ease when she was the driver rather than a passenger in a car. Her husband acquiesced and left the driving to her. She had little tolerance ever for riding in the back seat of a car. (I meant to ask her how she endures riding in taxicabs!)

Incidentally, Jane's decision to return from St. Louis prevented a rational discussion with the pilot. Still, so apprehensive about flying, Jane's emotional state ruled out a more reasonable solution.

In the seminar, Jane commented she would feel at ease if I were her pilot, which confirmed her uncertainties lessened when she was personally acquainted with authority figures in control. Humorously, I suggested she consider pre-flight meetings with the pilot each time, and "leave the flying to him." Eventually her own confidence would take over. But unfortunately, Jane's life is ruled by uncertainties and chronic doubting of others — unless they have gained her confidence.

VINCE: A Study In SEPARATION ANXIETY

Childhood fears may linger silently into adulthood and emerge inappropriately under stress. It is quite likely phobias stem from early traumas which have left "weak spots" in one's ability to adapt to later encounters with stress.

Vince, for example, who had attended a seminar, learned one day he had to attend an out-of-town sales meeting. Further, his boss had given him only two days notice to fly to Dallas. Although it was an important trip, Vince was irritated with the short notice, but he wouldn't dare express his displeasure. Assertiveness was foreign to his nature, which makes one wonder why he chose a career in selling.

On the morning of his departure, Vince had his wife drive him to the airport. Instead of going to the departure gate, he stayed in the lobby area and studied the passengers as they waited to board the plane. He stood there, as if dazed and detached from his mission to fly.

As the agent closed the jetway door, Vince felt a brief rush of relief. His dilemma was solved! But was it? Vince's moment of relief was short-lived. Now he had to face his boss; he had to explain why he missed the plane and the important business appointment in Dallas. His troubles grew. Additionally, he had to reveal to his wife that he had failed to fly — again. It wasn't his first aborted trip by air; surely, he needed some special help.

It was obvious he failed to apply even one of the techniques we had addressed earlier in the seminar. He simply froze, stood in silent numbness and deluded himself as he watched the plane depart. Escape from fear was paramount; taking control of his fear never occurred to Vince. These steps had been well rehearsed, but he was overwhelmed with apprehension.

His problem? Not a simple case of aerophobia, but with further probing, I learned the source of Vince's fear was a classic display of separation anxiety. It was as though Vince had been left by his mother on his first day of school and had suffered an attack of school phobia. His frightened, child-like fear surfaced as he entered the airport — alone. So much more work remained to be done.

Comparing Vince's actions to a child's timidity revealed why he acted as he did. His shy and passive attitude belied his apparent maturity. Vince was uneasy leaving home. Why? Separation from his loved-ones caused a vague feeling of finality, as if he were facing some certain tragic happening, and he might never see his family again!

Vince was obsessed with tragedy besetting him on an airplane; rational thought was beyond his capability when fear of separation was embedded so deeply in his psyche.

The solution rested in programming Vince systematically to fly. Initially he would be accompanied by his loved ones, then a "weaning" process would follow, limited to short flights with brief periods of separation from his family. Gradually, he'd be able to tolerate longer trips, with longer periods away from home.

He would stay in contact with his family through frequent phone calls to counter the dread of his loneliness.

Later, with mild medication, Vince was able to fly with his wife on a short, one-hour trip. He was still uneasy, but he didn't feel abandoned when accompanied by his wife.

The program for change in Vince's aerophobia is not a simple process of desensitization. Further counselling that will focus on his unassertive, passive-dependency has been recommended. So far, Vince has procrastinated in pursuing this course, suggesting added signs of avoidance. Perhaps he fears further failure, if and when he makes a serious effort to fly.

Vince's track record of immaturity suggests many personality weak spots must be strengthened to overcome his self-doubts, feelings of insecurity, and over-dependence on others, including loved ones. The prognosis for overcoming his anxiety related to separation is guarded at best, which limits the likelihood that Vince will ever fully overcome his fear of flying. His continued avoidance has resulted in the need to change jobs, limiting his employment to local sales only.

Vince is apparently willing to accept career limitations because of his self-imposed torment. The problem remains a concern to his family as well, which only adds to Vince's frustration.

Jane and Vince have lingering doubts about flying, which suggests that only marginal gains have been made. Added effort on their part may yield further improvement as many others have joyously discovered.

CAROLYN: A Case of Substance Abuse

Medicine for the treatment of the chronically ill, both physical and emotional, can produce dramatic benefits.

Chronic depressions diminish readily with proper anti- depressant medication, and anxieties decline in short order with a myriad of tranquilizers. The more serious mental disorders have diminished dramatically since the development of anti-psychotic drugs.

Even anticipated anxieties can be relieved with medication. Agoraphobia and panic disorders subside with proper medication together with supportive behavioral therapy.

Regardless, in symptomatic relief there is usually a price to pay in the form of side effects, which in some cases may be worse than the illness itself. Such is often the situation when tranquilizers are abused. A case in point.

Carolyn could manage to fly occasionally, but only on short trips. She found her anxiety barely tolerable with Valium, which dulled the sharp edge of her tension and anxiety in the air — for brief periods at least.

One wintry day, Carolyn and her husband made plans to escape the snowy blasts of the Midwest with a trip to Acapulco. Ideal weather, sunny beaches and a luxury hotel provided a strong incentive to fly, but the extended distance of the flight became a real problem: the fastest flight to Mexico was more than three hours.

Carolyn decided to tough it out. Her friend "Val" would get her through it. Her prescription called for 5mg. three times a day, which meant that her doctor allowed her a total of 15 mg. per day to curb her anxiety. Unfortunately, Carolyn measured anxiety in direct proportion to the amount of time she spent in flight.

The big day started with Carolyn taking one Valium as she awakened from a turbulent night's rest. She took another as she and her husband were leaving for the airport. As they entered the airport, Carolyn felt an added tinge of anxiety, and she dealt with the excitement by taking another pill! She was keeping count of her excesses, but still she defended the need for each one.

The flight was delayed for 40 minutes. (Flights are often late, and even if they aren't, the rush for on-time departure torments and tests most aerophobic's tolerance for confusion.) The wait became intolerable, so again, just 5 mg. more!

Finally after takeoff, Carolyn decided again to ease her anguish and increase her Valium intake; after all, challenging fate for three hours would require more than the usual dosage, so...

By now, you have the picture. Carolyn continued to overreact to each event of the trip. The flight was delightful for other passengers, but Carolyn continued to sense numerous bursts of periodic anxiety. When the plane door finally closed, when the engines started, when the plane roared on takeoff, when the landing gear doors made strange creaking sounds, when a slight ripple (or two) happened in the otherwise smooth air, when a child fussed or cried aloud, when a passenger stared at her — all these became unnerving stimuli which Carolyn saw as potential major disasters. All were normal sounds and sights, but there seemed to be no end to her agitated overreactions.

She remained "white-knuckled," terrified, irritable, jittery and tragically uptight during the entire trip. By her calculation, which her husband confirmed, she had taken at least eight of her "escape" pills, which far exceeded her prescribed **daily** dosage — in only **eight hours!**

Amazingly, all this medication had little effect in reducing her apprehension. For Carolyn, anxiety was a "large bolus of adrenaline," which she could not subdue otherwise.

On deplaning in Acapulco, Carolyn arrived at the foot of the loading steps under her own power, but when she set foot on the ground, she collapsed! Her husband simply had to pick her up and proceed through customs, to a waiting taxi, to the hotel, and to their room. He actually carried her, coma-like, all the way!

For more than 24 hours Carolyn remained sleeping soundly in a deep slumber. She had made it to Acapulco, but at what a price! Twenty-four hours of vacation were wasted in sleep , and she missed two full days of fun in the sun.

But that's only part of this unfortunate episode. Her stay in paradise was not enjoyable because of the real and anticipated anxiety she felt while agonizing over the return trip — a pathetic, no-win, self-defeating dilemma that besets many who are faced with an intense fear of flying, once they condescend to fly without learning to deal with their phobic reactions.

Carolyn now knew medication was not the answer. Sure, she flew, but with little gain over the irrational understanding of her problem. Her aerophobia was suggestive of certain "weak spots" in her makeup, which took the form of a pedantic, intense over-concern for trivial details and a compulsive need for vigilance against mishap. She lived in constant anticipation of adversity. The thought of flying found her to be obsessed with hazardous occurrences.

Much like Jane, Carolyn was not fearful of losing control of herself; she grew apprehensive and frustrated at not having some voice or control over external events that might adversely affect her, and her doubt of others was pervasive.

Normally, Carolyn was more than adequately assertive, but even that trait invited problems for her. Her feelings of irritability spread abrasively to others. In her anxious state, almost nothing pleased her. Neither sympathy nor understanding from others (even flight attendants) was accepted nor recognized; her husband, feeling helpless, could only insulate himself from her torment whenever they flew, which furthered her aggravations with his "benign neglect" of her.

So, defeated, Carolyn attended an aerophobia seminar. Soon she discovered her intensity about meaningless detail and her obsessive apprehension about some remote, vague happening which might befall her (or her loved ones). She typified the "what-if syndrome" by asking more doubting questions than any of the others in the seminar. She soon became aware of the absurdity of her many concerns.

I urged her to verbalize her concerns, rather than obsess over them. I encouraged her to ask, "What if the wing fell off?" if that was her burning concern. Her endless lists of "what-ifs" became humorous and provided laughs for her cohorts in the seminar. She soon phrased her concerns with a jovial chuckle, becoming less anxious with each question she asked. Carolyn's humor became infectious to all.

Carolyn can now laugh at herself. She can also shrug her shoulders more often. When she saw the value of being more "laid-back," her anxiety became tolerable. What relief!

"You can't beat humor or laughing for tension relief," says Norman Cousins, famous author, and now lecturer at UCLA Medical Center. He proposes that relief, if not "cure," is possible among the seriously ill by lifting their moods and spirits through the use of humor.

Carolyn became a good laugher, mostly at her own antics. Even now, when a baby cries, or a wing-flap motor hums ominously, Carolyn only grins. She won, simply by deferring her concern over trivia, and placing trust in the ability of others, especially the flight crews. Longer flights are now managed; stays are enjoyed without dreading the return flight, which is the greatest gain for Carolyn — and her husband!

Dave: Airsickness Arrested

There are other flying discomforts for which medication can provide relief, if taken properly. For example, nausea was once an agonizing problem for air passengers, although there is very little airsickness on jet flights of today.

The DC-3 for instance, was always equipped with quart-sized ice cream containers for the "passengers' comfort," when an attack of nausea erupted. In those years a part of the duty of the flight attendant (known as hostesses on TWA in the early days) was to see that a container was near-at-hand when needed and then discreetly discarded in a lavatory refuse bag. She then offered a minty-flavored gum to the embarrassed, indisposed passenger.

Today, airlines provide a small, flat plastic bag with a score card printed on it for use in gin rummy games. The bags are discarded now when the **scores** fill it. There's little else that ever fills them.

I don't intend to belittle the problem of airsickness. It is devastatingly embarrassing to the sufferer; relief is not easy once the sure signals of nausea begin. Emotions can play a role in gastric distress; excitement and fatigue can be factors, and they often are. Social concerns escalate with a queasy stomach.

Nevertheless, relief is usually available whether the cause of gastric upset is emotional, physical, or social. A passenger named Dave found airsickness relief much to his ecstatic delight.

Dave typified the Big-10 offensive tackle that he once was. He was also an All-American candidate who stood six- feet-four inches and weighed a muscular 245 pounds. Dave had flown many times, including flights to Bowl games with his teammates, friends and coaches, and he had never had a problem with airsickness, until later.

Now, fresh out of school, Dave embarked on a business career with a large insurance firm. He would surely be an executive one day, and it seemed nothing could interfere with his continued success. Nothing, that is, except he had acquired a sensitive gastric problem. Dave became particularly intolerant of the slightest bounces caused by air turbulence. Flying, which he once enjoyed, became a real concern now had become unnerving and threatened his future as a business executive.

No longer was he a raucous jock. He was now a young, uptight businessman, well-attired in a three-piece suit; a trip to the formidable home office frankly made him nervous. While he was on the plane, making just such a trip, his anxiety and tension heightened. The more he thought about what was expected of him in his business career, the tighter his muscles grew. The first ripple of turbulence found him fully braced as if meeting the onslaught of a charging linebacker. It triggered a gastric reflex, and he simply lost it all — explosively! Dave's dilemma was that he didn't know what to do about it, and humiliation limited his seeking help.

Later, Dave signed up and attended an aerophobia seminar. At first, perhaps because of his embarrassment, he failed to divulge his real reason for enrolling. The general seminar program addresses the problem of turbulence, but since nausea is seldom a problem with jet flying, we make little mention of air or motion sickness unless it is a particular problem for someone.

As we explain in the seminar, bracing the body during turbulence only intensifies the bounces. By relaxing deep in the seat, your body becomes a more efficient shock absorber.

Turbulence **is** an exaggerated concern of aerophobics, but for reasons which remain a mystery, more often their discomfort is defined as fear rather than as nausea. That was not the case with Dave.

As part of the program, we planned a flight two days after Dave's seminar. Dave had booked his fiance to accompany him on the trip for companion support. We planned a short trip to St. Louis to include lunch, viewing a TV football game in the TWA Ambassador Lounge, and a return trip that evening.

It would be a "no-pressure" flight, the kind so many other seminar participants had benefitted from with cohesive group support. On these therapeutic excursions, a team-like spirit always emerges that is a powerful force for mutual success.

At the conclusion of the seminar, Dave coyly called me aside to share a private concern: "Walt, the main reason I took this seminar is that I got damned tired of throwing up on my boss!" Reflexively, I laughed aloud, then with stifled amusement, I asked, "Why didn't you mention it before?" Dave admitted it was too embarrassing.

I went on, "Did you ever try any of the motion sickness medications?" He had tried some — but nothing had helped. Discouragement added to Dave's dilemma; he needed reassurance. Apprehension remained even after the seminar.

I assured him there was now another approach to the problem, which was more effective and definitely preferred when the oral medications were ineffective. I described it to him, much like a pharmaceutical salesman would do: a small, medicated, band-aid-like patch that is placed behind the ear would do the trick. It's nothing conspicuous. The drug is absorbed through the skin, which is a better pathway than the route through the stomach. My positive comments buoyed his hopes. He beamed with renewed hope and confidence as he went on describing, with a boyish grin, one of the occasions when he "spewed" on his boss. It was both sad and laughable. Just talking about his last trip served as a catharsis that afforded him a better understanding of the problem.

Dave called his physician to pick up the skin patches. He arrived for our flight, the picture of confidence, as he turned his head to display the patch behind his ear. He was ready for the test — the big game!

Boarding the flight was routine. Conversations were best describ- ed as light and humorous within the group. Smiles were in abundance as I scanned those in my view. Then, three minutes after takeoff, we encountered a few light bounces of choppy air and for an instant, my thoughts focused on the ex-jock turned executive, wondering how he was managing his fragile "tolerance of turbulence."

Just then, I clearly heard my name called out. I felt a hesitancy to acknowledge the call, but I did. Looking back two rows, I saw Dave, head and shoulders above the others, a broad grin filling his face. In a sturdy voice, his "Thanks Walt!" signalled instant relief — for both of us.

Dave enjoyed the rest of the trip as he had in his college days. His background as an athlete served him well in this situation. The seminar was his training ground. He learned the strategies for his "game plan" and was confident he could execute his assignment. He played his position well, astounded at the effectiveness of such a puny patch of plastic as it blocked his charging belly.

Or did it? I prefer to believe his insight and learning how to take charge of his tension and anxiety really accounted for much of his control. Still, I can't be sure.

With Dave's confidence restored, I couldn't fault him for conti- nuing to use the skin patch as a security blanket. Whatever is effec- tive gets my approval, but Dave hinted that the need for further patches could be unlikely since he had gained such valuable insight.

Unfortunately not all flying disorders can be resolved as simply as Dave's. His motivation and willingness to take on his fear, as an opponent, spelled the ultimate victory. And for Dave, it was even better than winning the Rose Bowl!

Norman: A Terminal Case of Claustrophobia.

Those who suffer from claustrophobia comprise a goodly number of those who fear flying. It is ironic that the airplane becomes a scapegoat and major source of anxiety among air avoiders. All of avia- tion suffers as a result. The airplane was so faulted by Norman, a strapping, hale and hardy 40 year-old, who enrolled in the aerophobia seminar. He complained of a disabling fear of flying and little else.

Throughout the seminar Norman sat quietly, responding only to direct questions. As a concluding event of the seminar, the group was to take a local scenic flight in a nineteen-passenger commuter airplane.

Mike Scheidt, the Chief Pilot of Air Midwest, had flown these groups before, uneventfully, with complete success. He related affably to all of the apprehensive passengers and would visit with them before each flight and answer their questions, instilling certain confidence in them. His "Captain's bearing and presence" was genuinely effective in easing their concerns.

When we left the Medical Center for the airport, I offered to have Norman and another person ride with me. Norman chose to ride with another member of the group whose car was roomier than my sporty hatchback. His change of plan appeared reasonable and suggested nothing more at the time.

Arriving at the airport, we gathered at the gate area and watched the ramp activities as the ground crew readied our airplane for flight. The passenger list consisted of nine clients from the seminar, including Norman, plus seven other friends or spouses.

The atmosphere was congenial with most of them chatting and laughing at one anothers' antics. Norman remained aloof and expressionless in the otherwise jovial group. There was no hint that anyone might "abort" our mission.

Norman boarded the slender-bodied plane and selected a front seat just opposite the loading door. I boarded last and sat across from him. Norman sat mute, although he was noticeably vigilant in scanning the cabin, especially the entry door area.

Soon, the cabin door was closed, the engines started, and we began taxiing to the takeoff runway some five minutes away. I was able to view all the passengers from my seat. The expressions on their faces were quite a contrast to Norman's furtive grimace. As we began to taxi, I announced I had brought a chilled bottle of champagne for those who would like to propose a short toast once we were aloft. I had chosen the moment carefully intending to provide a distraction, and it succeeded as their cheers drowned out the roar of the turbine engines. Levity was prevalent throughout the cabin, except for Norman.

As I glanced at Norman, he mumbled something barely audible, and I sensed he was uncomfortable. I leaned closer to hear him more clearly. Without raising his voice, he stated with slight emphasis, "I have to go back." His remark indicated a need for reassurance, which I offered by suggesting he try the six-second quieting exercise. "Time for the smile, breathe and relax bit," I replied in a consoling tone of voice.

Norman stared at me sphinx-like with a stern expression. He then restated with more firmness in his voice, "Take me back!" I assured him I didn't think that would be necessary if he would make an effort to relax and calm his body. I made firm eye contact with him to determine if his facial gestures were those of fear or anger. I was uncertain which emotion ruled his reaction, but I began the relaxation process to divert him from his self-induced stress. It failed.

"Please, take me back," he said with a more demanding, even threatening tone of voice. Visions of the "showdown at the OK corral" flashed before my eyes. I steadied my stare, straight-in-the-eye as Gary Cooper might have played the role, but I had serious doubts that I could "outdraw" Norman, or contain whatever impulsive action he might take.

Strategy called for a shift in plans as the plane continued to taxi. I reached for Norman's wrist, saying, "I want to check your pulse." He refused to extend his arm, so I leaned closer to him. His pulse was a strong 120 thumps a minute. He was tense; he kept eyeing the cabin door, which disturbed me. If he tried to exit with the plane moving — with the engines running — it could prove tragic.

To buy more time, I had to deny his demands. I then told him the decision to return and let him deplane would be made only if he calmed down. I considered it a mistake for him to **escape** at the peak of his anxiety. By escaping, he would only be rewarding his failure. He was so very close to proving to himself he could manage his painful dread if he would only endure for a few more minutes.

I rechecked his pulse; it had slowed only slightly. His facial and verbal expressions suggested he remained determined to gain his freedom, physically.

I signalled Captain Scheidt to delay the takeoff until we resolved a problem. With the plane parked near the takeoff position, I insisted that Norman "cool down." I had another card to play as I stated firmly we would not take him back until he became more relaxed and calm, as evidenced by a lowered pulse. My voice tone was firm. I fixed eye contact with him, and he bought it, for the moment.

The others studied this encounter, though not fully able to hear our comments. Fortunately, they remained unaffected by his reluctant behavior. After some few minutes, Norman appeared calmer; his pulse rate was now just under 100 sturdy beats per minute. He had done well and I commended him. But then, I pondered, what might result if I nodded to Captain Scheidt to take off? Would the benefit be worth the risk? I had serious doubts and was unwilling to gamble on the outcome.

I then asked Norman if he would just "give it a try," but he was firm in his demand, saying "No, take me back!"

Sensing defeat, I agreed. We returned and he got off. As we were taxiing back to the terminal, I told him I was sorry I had failed him. There was so much more to be done by both of us. He agreed, but unfortunately, I detected a sense of relief, not remorse. Too bad; his fear can only persist!

You may be curious about the effect of this episode on the others, and I admit it did give me considerable concern at the time. The impact on the group was nil! Not one of them showed any sign of weakening in their resolve to fly.

In fact, after we let Norman off at the ramp and taxied out once again, a crescendo of camaraderie spread throughout the cabin, and a warm feeling of solidarity prevailed. If anything, there was a sense of relief from witnessing someone more frightened than they were. Now, they grew confident in their separate victories.

The cabin atmosphere was more like that of a group of students on a field trip to Disneyland in anticipation of a fun-filled time. They were not disappointed. The champagne added to their enjoyment of the flight. They even drank a toast to Norman!

The sequel to this situation is even more astonishing as Norman called me later that evening. Apologetically, he related a mind-baffling tale. He had previously flown in an open cockpit biplane while the pilot stunted through loops and rolls — spinning toward Earth — with no ill-effects! He had even gone "hang gliding" several times!

Heights or falling through space didn't bother Norman, which may sound like a strange and confusing paradox for an aerophobic. The only answer I could find was that I had made a misdiagnosis. Norman was not aerophobic!

Then the mystery unravelled. Norman suffered from a severe case of **claustrophobia,** which explained his hesitation to be crowded in the back seat of my two-door sports car. To him, closed-off spaces were certain death traps. The narrow, tube-like plane was too "tomb-like" to allow Norman the needed free space for breathing. Flying in a closed cabin was nothing like the freedom of floating aloft while bridled only in a hang glider. Like an eagle, he felt free, but in any tight enclosure, such as he experienced in the narrow commuter plane, he felt trapped.

Since Norman had disguised the intensity of his claustrophobia, the seminar agenda did not provide him with the time to desensitize his feelings of encapsulation. Had I known this clearly during the seminar, I would have impressed upon him the need for a more gradual, and varied exposure to become more tolerant of conditions he found uncomfortably constricting (such as the backseat of a car, and yes, even closed elevators were dreaded).

Norman's symptoms were familiar to me since I have had to conquer similar feelings of claustrophobia (as I recall my bouts with oxygen masks). It takes precise planning, gradual exposure and time. Norman was rushed; we had bypassed several important intermediate steps, leaving him hopelessly ill-prepared to contain his claustrophobic reactions.

My concluding remarks to Norman suggested he would have done much better if we had let him ride on the wing of the plane. He agreed, simply saying, "Yep!"

Too often we fault the airplane or other problems we encounter in air travel for causing "the agony of aerophobia" when we overlook the actual contributing factors which are most often, **far removed from flying!**

Dick: Fear Defused

A year later, I encountered a similar situation on a group flight to St. Louis, but it had a vastly different outcome, I'm pleased to relate.

Dick, was a 44-year-old machinery salesman, sports car enthusiast and a Navy veteran. He was apparently well-travelled, having sailed abroad on a European tour, but he had never flown!

Unlike Norman, he freely expressed his discomfort with claustrophobia he was certain would make flying unbearable for him. But there was more to his story.

Dick was an excellent driver, and high speeds in a car held no threat to him — as long as he was driving. At any speed, with another person driving, he was ill-at-ease. The thought of flying with someone else in control was inconceivable. He had even considered learning to fly, but he soon dismissed the idea as not a workable approach to his problem.

Dick was doubly hindered, first by his claustrophobia, and second by his need for being in control of his destiny when it came to vehicles. He developed a strong incentive to overcome his fear of flying when his fiance moved to Chicago.

Dick would spend a tiring twenty hours (round trip) driving on weekends to carry on the courtship, and it was wearing heavily on their enjoyment of each other. It wasn't fair his fiance should fly for all their meetings, but he simply was unable to take turns in making flights.

The long-distance affair was rapidly deteriorating directly attributable to his dread of the air. Dick soon became motivated to seek help and enrolled in the aerophobia seminar.

At the conclusion of the seminar, we planned a group flight as usual from Kansas City to St. Louis. Dick felt he was prepared to make his maiden air voyage along with fourteen others who had completed the program. He alone, had never flown before.

After we boarded the plane in Kansas City, I found a seat next to Dick. He scanned about the seat area, studying his seat belt, glancing out of the window and adjusting air vents. He was quiet but tense. An engine started while we were still parked at the gate. As the drone of the engine broke the silence in the cabin, Dick uttered, "I can't do it!"

His remark and serious tone of voice caught me off guard. I smiled faintly at him and said, "good timing!" My reply puzzled him, which gave me a moment to clarify my reference to his timeliness or, rather, his lack of it.

After all, he had managed five minutes with the door closed, without becoming unnerved, and he had done well. His reaction to the engine rumbling sounds was explainable, so I commented on that to distract him further. I trusted my remarks would explain his unsettled feelings by commenting on the strangeness of the jet engine sounds that were a totally new hearing sensation. I then added some other casual remarks I hoped would stimulate his reasoning ability. It worked, and I was able to buy another two or three minutes. By this time, another engine started and its noises blended in with the first. Slowly, the airplane began to move from the gate. Continued distraction was my game plan.

Dick studied my every word with difficulty, struggling to draw a logical conclusion while in his tense, confused state. Then, turning his attention to more immediate concerns, he wiped the "cold sweat" from his brow, but his hand was dry! That he felt drenched with sweat even though he wasn't sweating, suggested it was time for the smile-breathe-relax diversion exercise. It was time to stifle his anxiety with the techniques he had rehearsed in the seminar.

Dick managed a feeble smile, but that was all. He then resorted to a valiant effort to assure me that getting off the airplane was his only salvation. He insisted his heart was "running wild" and that his father had died of a heart attack. He was certain he was destined to the same fate, and it would surely occur any minute!

Continuing the strategy of buying time and distracting Dick, I checked his pulse and gained another valuable minute. Time was important since the airplane was progressing to the runway. All the while, my assessment of the problem dictated I stay the course with Dick and see him through his first takeoff.

Dick noted the movement of the airplane as he glanced out the window. Again he asserted he wasn't going to make it, saying, "Stop them and take me back, or I'll stop them!" With this threat, his pupils grew larger, and his voice was firm. He tried to be convincing with his every expression, but I sensed a difference from Norman's challenge. I would not concede defeat and give in this time.

He needed more diversion, so I placed my hand on his chest to check his "pounding heart." It was visibly thumping, but I acted unimpressed. I gained further distraction by directing his attention to the movement and acceleration of the plane, and then saying, "Dick, the takeoff will be smoother and slower than your turbocharged Laser." He challenged my remark, which revealed that he was again misdirected from his agony. Another precious minute was gained.

While he questioned the subject of jet acceleration, I continued the discussion with a comment that he was certain "jets zoomed" off the ground, but he would be amazed how smooth it would be. Dick's puzzlement at how a car could have a greater acceleration than a jet plane busied his attention from his pounding chest. A car faster? No way! Impossible, or was it? (P.S. a car is faster in initial acceleration up to 100 to 120 mph, but then the jet plane will leave any land vehicle behind.)

The acceleration gambit did the trick. Getting off the plane was not possible now because we were nearing the takeoff runway. Suddenly, Dick blurted, "I know what you're doing Walt, and it won't work. I've got to get off, now!" I chuckled aloud, thinking a silent smile alone wouldn't work, and I continued humorously: "Dick, you've passed the peak; it's just like Chuck Yeager breaking the sound barrier. It's down hill from here, and you've won the battle!"

The 727 gently started its takeoff run. Sensing defeat, Dick now had to trust me and believe that the worst was over — and it was! As the engines grew louder, his knuckles blanched whiter, then, as he loosened his grip on the arm rest, he became less tense and began to accept his fate — he was committed to fly.

As the takeoff progressed, I described the event with a play-by-play dialogue that held his attention. Dick felt the lift-off and groaned softly through his clenched teeth; then he quietly restated his trust in me. As he sensed a letdown in his body bracing, he managed a faint grin. Shortly, Dick initiated the smile-breathe-relax bit — on his own! A deeper smile grew with each breath cycle. Soon, with a broad grin, he uttered softly, "Walt, I can even wiggle my toes!" We both laughed heartily.

Clinically, I learned a great deal from that ten-minute episode. I had just witnessed a full-blown "implosive reaction," an interesting psychological term describing a catastrophic, internal reaction that occurs as a consequence of intense fear. Dick's reactions were classic — precisely as described in the text books.

Implosion therapy is a technique used by some therapists in treating phobias. It forces exposure. It's like throwing someone off a high-diving platform to achieve the feeling of relief that comes as a reward for the person emerging safely after the devastating plunge. In such an exposure crisis the emotions become flooded, but once the threat eases, the overwhelming fear should subside, that is, if all goes well!

Fear should fade as anxiety abates if one can endure the peaking of an emotional crisis. The Chuck Yeager analogy is accurate, and it was effective in containing Dick for a valuable instant, for which he remains ever grateful.

Although I favor a more gradual exposure than subjecting a person to an intentional implosive experience (even though it has often proved effective in research studies), it is difficult to avoid in those persons with a lowered tolerance for stress when they are forced to endure a feared situation.

Implosive therapy is a tougher course, but then at times, a successful outcome may be worth the momentary stress, as it was in Dick's case. He survived his internal catastrophe with great relief at its passing as the threat faded. He was justifiably jubilant in his victory.

On the return flight, Dick actually gave the impression he was a veteran air traveller with his newly found confidence. His commuting love affair blossomed again, and vacation trips that he had avoided in the past were now in his plans once he had "toughed it out" and conquered the fear barrier!

I often wonder if Norman stayed the distance, like Dick, would he have calmed his claustrophobic reactions? I suppose I'll never know because he made good his escape. It may be too much for Norman ever to endure such torment. Although he tolerated open cockpit planes and hang gliders, he is still grounded from today's commercial air travel.

Carl: A Disabling Fear of Heights (Acrophobia)

After we had conducted several seminars, an unusual problem surfaced with the first case that was recognized as directly attributable to acrophobia. Fear of heights is not an uncommon fear. In fact, a strong case could be made for a universal uneasiness whenever we are physically exposed to lofty heights.

Fear of heights most likely involves a fear of falling or feelings of a lack of **visual support** when we are openly exposed in high places. The view through a ceiling-to-floor window from a high-rise building is a startling experience for many. The feeling of visual openness in modern, glass-enclosed elevators that provide a "bird's-eye-view" for riders is panic-producing for some. The fearful feeling is less intense if the window is above waist-level, which provides a more secure feeling of support.

Accordingly, there should be little concern for the "sense of height" when seated securely in an airplane. Even when one peers down, the visual space is limited and physical support should not be a problem when comfortably seated.

Acrophobia may have a transient influence while in flight, but I do not view it as central to the problem of aerophobia among those in the seminars, unless the "thought of height" is an obsession with them; another example of "thought impacting feeling!"

For example, Carl was a 42-year old management-level businessman who had mentioned his fear of heights only casually in the seminar. As his group gathered at the TWA Training Center for a tour of the simulators, we proceeded to the second floor by elevator. Next, we were to continue to the eighth floor for the simulation of flight in a cabin trainer. While awaiting the elevator, I noted Carl lingering behind, a gray-pallored expression on his face. I sensed a problem.

I eased my way to him, unobtrusively. With restraint in his voice, Carl advised that he would wait in the lobby and forego the trip to the eighth floor. For him, the thought of being any higher in the building was unbearable.

Carl had never been traumatized in a skyscraper incident other than perhaps reacting to one of the terror spectacle movies that depicted a holocaust in a high-rise structure. He could not account for the source of his intense feeling of dread. He admitted that he had long-been devastatingly ill-at-ease in tall buildings. His heart would race and pound; he ran short of breath and would tremble uncontrollably. These symptoms are all evidence of a near-panic state reaction resulting from his uncontrolled anxiety.

Others in the group soon became aware of Carl's quandary. Their encouragement was to no avail; he insisted that he would wait for them in the lobby.

At this juncture, I conducted a group discussion of the desensitizing process. Carl felt uneasy but attended to my comments that took on an air of "negotiations" for him to consider. He was not naive. He saw through my ploy and was dubious about his ability to proceed without greater risk of embarrassment.

Sensing his dilemma, I then mentioned his anticipated anxiety and assured him that he would do well if we went to the third floor and practiced some "conditioning." We could then continue in stages to the eighth floor for no more than a brief stay. He pondered my logic while I suggested that the group continue to the eighth floor and I would soon join them.

Soon, Carl and I were alone. It became apparent he had severely limited his living because of this "handicap dread of heights" that he had been unable to conquer. He admitted to career limitations and that he had lost untold opportunities for advancement. Embarrassment was constant when he had to refuse to ascend above the second floor of any building. He was depressed, angry, and tired, but left with little hope for any change.

I offered a "one-on-one" try to put an end to his problem if he would bear with me. He accepted the offer.

I described his reaction as a result of a "flooding" of emotion that we could capitalize on. The principle of stress inoculation was outlined: he would visualize the terror of being on the next floor and deal with it until it subsided. Then, a step at a time, we would proceed to the next floor — even if it took the night to tolerate the exposure!

The game plan was set to use the relaxation exercise to cope with whatever stress he encountered. Concentration on the calming effects served to distract him from his anxiety and the embarrassment he felt for leaving the group. First, we would walk up to the third floor, assess the level of fear and work on that. On his approval, we would continue. He was to be in control; he could alter the course to ease his condition. Carl managed a grin as we approached the stairs.

On the third floor, we gazed at the street below while Carl checked his pulse, at first racing wildly, then slowing, slowly. I commented on his relaxed facial expression as he regulated his breathing. I praised his control and suggested we look around at some of the classrooms and make a trip to the men's room to freshen up. His composure grew.

I left the choice to Carl to continue to the fourth floor or take the elevator to a higher floor. He pondered his option with a stern expression that soon evaporated to a childish grin as he said unhesitatingly, "Let's join the group!"

I sensed a rush of victory, but hesitated, then firmly grasped his arm as I commended him and explained I understood full well the courage he was displaying. I assured him the worst was over, at least for the moment. He had dealt with his social embarrassment, he had control of his thoughts and feelings, and his anxiety became manageable. More so, he had "broken the fear barrier" just as Chuck Yeager had done. We signalled the elevator.

As we stepped off the elevator at the eighth floor, a well-deserved burst of applause greeted us. The group spirit was clear evidence of a desire to share in Carl's victory.

Carl was obsessed with a fear of heights in public buildings, which had kept him from flying since many air terminals were multi-level. Carl had flown, and he admitted that airplane height did not hold the same threat for him that even three or four-story buildings had caused him. The terror became manageable only when Carl learned to divert his obsessive thoughts and calm his physical reactions. Avoidance was ended, for one time at least, and Carl's prospects had brightened. He is intent on continuing the adjustment to high-rise structures; flying is a cinch!

Ellen: Rewarded Efforts

Ellen typified many of those successful women in the seminars who were the affluent wives of successful business or professional men. She was bright, outgoing and creative. Her husband, a professional, was sensitive to her discomfort and dread of flying, a concern that is not always prevalent among the spouses of aerophobics. Marital strife often erupts when a spouse is less than sympathetic and supportive in helping a mate overcome certain emotional distresses.

Ellen was blessed with an understanding husband who made frequent trips abroad in the conduct of his business. She had grown tired of missing out on annual trips to Europe because of her acknowledged irrational fear of flying. Even when she relented and did fly, Ellen could not enjoy vacations in exotic resort areas because of her agonizing over the return flight; a pathetic affair which she was determined to change.

Ellen approached the rationale of the seminar with the usual aerophobic's skepticism and doubt. Once it became clear her undue concern and apprehension were pervasive, she became aware of the role negative attitudes played in her anxiety-riddled life.

As Ellen's perception of her problem became more clear to her, she became curious about the idea that she could take control of her negative feelings by applying the techniques of biofeedback relaxation and a planned distraction from her anxious thoughts and discomforting feelings while flying. Motivation to overcome her fear of flying increased as her husband continued his tactful encouragement.

We planned a flight to San Francisco for her in order to test the effectiveness of the seminar. Armed with some paper work for balancing her checkbook, a deck of cards for playing gin rummy with her husband, and finally a tape recorder for listening to the relaxation tape from the seminar, Ellen paraded on board the plane with considerably less concern than ever before. Would it work? She hoped it would, but more important, Ellen was prepared to make every effort to endure and overcome her undue anguish.

With sufficient motivation and a game plan in mind, Ellen was determined to allay all fear of having an anxiety attack while flying. She felt a calm now that had eluded her on every previous flight. She was ecstatic with her newly found composure while flying.

On their return to Kansas City, Ellen felt compelled to call me (apologetically, at a late-night hour) to share in her achievement. She commented pridefully, "I never dreamed that I would be able to sleep on an airplane — I fell sound asleep thirty minutes after takeoff and even slept through the dinner!" Ellen's husband was even more appreciative of her accomplishment.

They now share the annual tour to Europe in a manner they never before thought possible. They have become "true ambassadors" of air travel.

Although these are isolated examples, they do represent a cross-section of the symptoms and problems that are related to an irrational fear of air travel. Actually, the majority of the participants in the seminars with similar symptoms have been successful in flying with significant decreases in their overall anxiety. Most of these problems are solvable with intensive effort on the part of both client and clinician.

Successes or failures in outcome are best when shared, and as their "flight instructor," I revel with those in their victories and refuse to despair for those who appear to suffer defeat. I am optimistic that a willingness for extra effort is the ultimate solution in those cases that remain in question. I trust they too, will **not** despair.

Chapter 7

GAINING CONTROL OF FEAR

I believe that anyone can conquer fear by doing the things he fears to do, provided he keeps doing them until he gets a record of successful experiences behind him.

Eleanor Roosevelt.

The above quotation is a credit to the astuteness and remarkable insight of a former first lady. It's an interesting corollary to the more famous statement by her husband, President Franklin D. Roosevelt: *The only thing we have to fear is fear itself!*

At first glance it appears that Eleanor Roosevelt knew the basic principles of **systematic desensitization**, a method that gradually reduces fear by a protected, repeated exposure to the feared situation.

Over a period of **protected exposure**, the levels of fear and sensitivity will diminish. This is a **conditioning** process familiar to psychologists who subscribe to the principles of learning theory which state that behaviors acquired as learned responses can be modified or extinguished by a process of **relearning** or **unlearning**.

As stated earlier, some fears are instinctive, but most are learned. Psychologists generally consider specific fears are learned. The challenge then becomes that of overcoming irrational fears that interfere with our enjoyment of living.

Fear is a **stimulus** that influences behavioral **responses**. In this context, behavior modification has become a favored treatment among psychologists dealing with phobic disorders. A look at some of the assumptions and techniques of "Stimulus-Response Learning Theory" will help in gaining an understanding of the rationale used in treating phobias.

Changing Behavior

Habit is habit and not to be flung out of the window by any man, but coaxed downstairs a step at a time.

Mark Twain

Extinction of fear is best accomplished gradually, over a reasonable period. Some fears diminish easily. It is unlikely any fear will ever be overcome without some measure of **exposure, encounter** or **confrontation** of the feared situation!

Some fears leave in one quick-fix exposure by the person attacking that which is feared. This approach is known as the "counterphobic" method of extinction. For example, if one fears heights and falling, the remedy would be to — take up skydiving! Sounds harsh, but it is often effective in allaying a fear of sky-diving. But one may still retain remnants of uneasiness related to height exposure while looking over a high ledge, with or without a parachute!

A gradual exposure to a specific fear is more practical. The saying, "Life by the yard is hard; by the inch, it's a cinch," holds quite true. Systematically desensitizing a person in a **controlled, protective** and **reassuring** procedure offers a far more palatable means of modifying fear. Here's an example of a learned fear and its subsequent extinction.

Almost any baby would enjoy a soft, furry, toy animal as a pleasant stimulus. If such a toy is given to a baby together with a startling loud noise (unpleasant stimulus), the toy is then associated with the fearful response and becomes a feared object.

When the toy is presented again, it is likely to produce a startle reaction, even though the noise is not repeated. The infant has become conditioned (sensitized) to fear the toy by association.

If presenting the toy subsequently produces agitation (in the absence of the noise), one may conclude the baby has learned to fear the toy.

To modify this agitated response systematically, the toy must be reintroduced to a position where the baby recognizes the toy, reacts, but soon calms when the noise is absent. The toy can then be left for a period to provide for **adaptation** to the now, non-threatening toy.

Gradually, the toy can be moved closer and closer until the agitation fades. Ultimately the baby can be expected to accept the toy with pleasure. Some infants, for unknown reasons, may remain ever skeptical and vigilant. Could this concern be an early indication of chronic doubting and mistrust? We can only speculate.

The conditioning process can be accelerated by the use of a **reward** or a **distraction**. For example, when the baby is involved in a comforting activity (such as feeding), the toy may be re-introduced with less threat, simply because of the pleasurable distraction of feeding. Voila! The sting of fear is extinguished!

I suggest a fear of flying comes about in the same way the baby mistakenly learned to fear the furry toy. A potpourri of noises and unexplained happenings frequently associated with flying may easily startle the anxious passenger into his fearful state.

Maturation into adulthood is of little help. Unexpected and unexplained events on airplanes (including unusual sounds) incite startle reactions in those already apprehensive while aloft in an airplane. Unjustly, flying takes the blame (a bum rap!) because it is the flight itself that is identified as the source of discomfort.

In defense of a multiplicity of causes for the onset of aerophobia, I would point out that an untold number of potential contributing factors exists. For example, **internal** physical conditions may trigger a fearful reaction much like the odd noises and other **external** factors.

Aerophobia, like agoraphobia, often stems from a fear of public embarrassment if self-control is lost. The numbers attending the aerophobia seminars that are so affected are sufficient to see aerophobia as a social phobia.

But then, man as a social being has a tremendous capacity for adaptation. Consider the adjustment required of the newborn at birth.

The fetus, conditioned to the security and warmth in the womb, is then forced (painfully?) into the narrowed birth canal (could this aspect of birth be the origin of claustrophobia?) before exiting into a cold, outer world. Serenity is ended with startling severity. The baby is forever separated from the comforting environs of the womb (could birth be the origin of separation anxiety?) and is forcibly made to adapt.

Such is the "birth trauma" story, so familiar to many psychological researchers; an event we all have had to endure. Avoidance is impossible, but is it possible the trauma of birth is the source of all anxiety as certain theorists believe? This view is another example of psychological theory that remains open to debate and more speculation, while being difficult to disprove.

Are the neuroses a consequence of an occasional inability to adapt to such an early trauma? Many persons are faced with a lifetime of neurotic maladjustment, but for others, adjustment is no problem. Adapting to a stressful environment varies widely.

Workers adjust to many undesirable conditions over varying periods of exposure. Harsh noises, extremes of bothersome stimuli (heat, cold, odors, dampness etc.) are adapted to in time by our natural ability to acclimate to environmental extremes.

A friend once commented, "We can adjust to anything — even hanging — if we hang long enough!" Yes, if need be, the body is remarkably adaptive, given the exposure, and a measure of tolerance!

First Aid For Fear: The Importance of Breathing

The body's reaction to fear is reflexive and instantaneous. Shortness of breath is often the first sign of impending doom, the sequel of which is a variety of feelings — rapid pulse, dizziness, choking sensation, cold sweats, tremors, stomach flutters, or even chest pains — that only fuel the fire of fear.

Normally, breathing is left to our reflexes, so much so, we are seldom aware of the respiratory process, even when there is a disturbance in the air flow that deprives us of the "breath of life." Hence, breath control must be viewed as the first line of defense in combatting the stresses of anxiety or fear. But first, we must be aware of the need for regulating our breathing — consciously!

To **SMILE, BREATHE,** and **RELAX** takes but a few seconds, and the body may react as though it is under less threat in an equally brief few seconds. Precious calming begins. Our senses may even clear as stress reduces, and we **learn** to contain these **reflexes of fear.**

Internal changes occur similarly with pleasant feelings as they do with unpleasantries. Smiling suggests a pleasant state to the watchdog endocrine system, and a grin is better than a grimace for misdirecting and silencing a fear alarm! Further calm continues. A smile, followed by a slow, deep breath and by relaxing our muscles as we exhale brings about amazing physical quieting in short order. Some trainers in stress management have labelled this simple procedure the "six-second quieting response," which can bring precious relief in such a brief expanse of time.

Those attending the aerophobia seminar are encouraged to use the **smile, breathe,** and **relax** procedure at any time they feel tense or anxious: after a disturbing phone conversation, during a tension-filled meeting with the boss, even frustrations felt while driving in heavy traffic can be eased by taking the six-second break while pausing at a stop signal. Again, awareness of the need for proper breathing is the key to stress, tension and fear reduction. Try it and savor the relief that is inevitable.

Overcoming Fear: Put on a Happy Face

Gaining control over fear is not a simple process. It isn't like learning the multiplication tables. Ideally, a plan should be devised for eventual exposure to the feared situation. Remember, **avoidance will only prolong the fear.**

The goal of gaining control over fear is most readily achieved by rational management of the "fight or flight" reaction. Once you accomplish that task, subsequent encounters should offer less threat, and you should be able to tolerate them handily in accordance with the basic principles of adaptation and conditioning.

You can make the exposure process to a feared situation more palatable by dividing it into four preparatory stages:

1) **VISUALIZE** performing the act. Imagine yourself in a calmed state while being exposed to your fear. Use positive thoughts to reinforce your achievement; say to yourself with certainty, **"I can remain calm and under control in an airplane."**

The foremost positive thinker, Harry Emerson Fosdick advises: "Hold a picture of yourself long and steadily enough in your mind's eye and you will be drawn toward it. Great living always begins with a picture held in your imagination of what you would like to do or be."

Expert golfers visualize their movements before each swing of the club. Even average golf enthusiasts have improved their game by picturing how they might play certain golf shots. A Vietnam POW veteran visualized playing golf throughout his six-year imprisonment — and won the first golf tournament he entered after his return home!

More remarkably, Charley Plumb, Navy pilot, spent his six-year POW internment learning to play the piano "on an imagined 3-octave keyboard scratched on a plank of wood!" His visual imagery was so vivid he could even "hear" a missed note — what an effective use of imagination as a "constructive compromise" and escape from a dreadful experience! His piano skills continue to provide many pleasant diversions from the demands of a fast-paced, public speaking schedule. The use of controlled fantasy and delusion aided his survival and served to shorten the interminable stress that was felt by all of the POWs. Certainly, visualizing a more pleasant activity can be an effective antidote for whatever stress or fear is felt while flying.

Advocates of visual imagery feel strongly that visualization provides a key to the sub-conscious with marked behavioral influences. While fearful thoughts excite, imagining pleasurable events calms. Is there any more relaxing escape than imagining a hole in one golf shot or a favorite musical rendition when caught up in a stressful plight — or flight?

2) **SIMULATE** exposure with trial runs. Visit the airport. Sit in an available plane and familiarize yourself with the routines of airport procedures. Have dinner at the airport with a friend. Act as if you were awaiting the departure of your flight! With calmed thoughts, sense and cultivate a casual, relaxed feeling. In this setting, your anxiety will ease and soon diminish.

3) **INITIATE** by choosing a short-duration flight with the help of your spouse, friend, or with a clinician-led group of other fearful flyers. Group flights are quite successful because of the shared encouragement and collective support that is generated among the participants.

Humorously, the notion that misery loves company becomes a central theme for the groups in the seminars.

Some consider use of a mild tranquilizer, when prescribed by their physician to ease the anxiety. As their psychologist, I sanction a prudent use of medication for initial trials, if it helps the resolve to fly, rather than avoid and not fly. Total dependency on medication is to be avoided. Some find alcohol eases their concerns. One or two drinks, if found to calm, may be acceptable, but more than two might be detrimental and is **not** recommended!

4) **PARTICIPATE** in subsequent trips as your fear subsides. You should derive more and more pleasure from flying on short, enjoyable trips. Praise **yourself** for **your** accomplishments and whatever mastery you achieve over your fears. You are not seeking instant bliss, rather,

you are striving to feel less stress and to be able to cope with that level of stress! Reducing stress is a good measure of your success, and such success will be rewarded by subsequent successes!

In working with aerophobics, there is one overriding axiom that confirms a sound principle of learning theory: **Do not reward failure!** Avoidance or escape is failure, and one should never reward either. Self-gain, even of the slightest measure is to be commended.

On completing a successful flight with a group of aerophobia sufferers, I require all participants congratulate one another. No one is allowed to "kiss the ground" after landing! The participants themselves deserve the credit, and they should share their bliss with those earnestly concerned with their accomplishment.

Persistence will penetrate the fear barrier. When fear peaks, a gradual calming will follow according to the principles of stress-adaptation. It helps to **anticipate this lessening of fear and sense the changes in your body** as the calmness sets in. Focus on that feeling: the relief, which is certain to come, as Chuck Yeager experienced with the calming in his body after breaking the sound barrier — pure ecstasy — the joy of conquest!

For those who persist in the avoidance of flying, I hold little optimism for their ever achieving the pleasures (and conveniences) that are possible in air travel. Those avoiding such stress will continue to be vulnerable to the ravages of fear until they take positive action to develop the art of stress management. Here's a starting point.

Stress Inoculation

In stress-management programs there is a technique called "Stress Inoculation." This technique is effective for coping with stressful events in advance, much like the principle of vaccination against a disease. The disease, in this case obviously, is stress.

The inoculation process entails **anticipation** of the stressful event, which is no problem for phobics because they live constantly in anticipation of fearful encounters.

Preparation and **awareness** are the keys to the prevention of overstress. Perceiving the problem with a **positive attitude plan** for coping with the stressful event is a must. There is an effective outline in problem solving much like the plan for exposure to flying. Here is such a plan for managing stress in advance of the event:

1) **ANTICIPATE** the expected stressor. Inoculation is achieved by visualizing the feared event and assigning a number to it from one to ten; that is, if it is expected to be severely disturbing, it is worth a ten; a moderate fear, a six or seven; a mild concern, something less.

2) **PLAN POSITIVELY** to **handle the stress** reaction. Imagine the encounter as vividly as possible while sensing the degree of expected discomfort. Consider possible options or strategies for dealing with the dilemma. Distraction by a pleasant task is effective.

For example, many see THE TAKEOFF as frighteningly unbearable. Knuckles blanch the whitest as the engine noise builds and the plane rumbles down the runway.

A workable plan for distraction is to **calculate the number of seconds** from the start of the engines' roar on the takeoff roll, until the plane leaves the runway. Counting, silently or aloud, or focusing on the sweep second hand of your watch (usually only 20 to 50 seconds), will be sufficient to divert your attention from the anguish sensed while becoming airborne.

Note: **Expect some anxiety** to occur! Remain confident of managing whatever intensity of stress you might feel. You are now in control to execute your coping strategy.

3) **PREPARE** for coping. Rehearsal and simulation are encouraged. For instance, if public speaking is a stressful situation, deliver your speech in private. Become familiar with the topic and test your reactions generated in a non-threatening atmosphere. Replace **dread** and **doubt** with **knowledge** and **confidence**.

Develop a degree of self-reliance in the mechanics of the encounter. Visualize the bodily changes in the controlled setting. Be aware anxiety is to be expected, but be confident of managing whatever level of anxiety is actually experienced. **EXPECT THE UNEXPECTED! BE FLEXIBLE!** And of greater importance, be **CONFIDENT!** You can cope!

4) **PRAISE YOURSELF**. When the encounter occurs, compare the impact felt to the anticipated degree of alarm. If it's more distressing than expected, commend your effort, courage, and persistence in confronting the situation. Self-praise is reassuring.

Continue the rehearsed strategies for coping. Remember your tension will peak, then subside. Fear and tension do not remain constant. Relaxation reduces tension.

If the encounter is **less stressful** than anticipated, your efforts are rewarded with a positive measure of success.

The real value of this exercise lies in the tendency for us to anticipate fear excessively. Imagining the worst but meeting the challenge and managing it, is gratifying. Your sense of achievement bolsters your confidence.

It is important to understand that the dread experienced in a phobic situation "does not remain constant!" The feelings of fear fluctuate in intensity, peaking with the more fearful thoughts, and subsiding with confident thoughts. Take note of the letup in the fear-induced reactions, and focus on the pleasurable sense of relief, which is sustainable with positive thoughts.

Dreaded illnesses have diminished under similar principles of inoculation. The impact of fear can be cushioned by the awareness that we can handle the stresses of fear — a rewarding discovery.

Autogenic Relaxation: Gaining Self-Control

We can dull the sting of fear when we make the nervous system an ally instead of an adversary.

We can enhance the self-concept by developing a greater awareness and acceptance of ourselves. Feelings of self-reliance generate confidence in our collective ability to manage stress. Understanding our reactions allows us a greater measure of management of our reactions to stress.

Autogenic relaxation permits a self-generated reduction of tension. The method for inducing a relaxed state using autogenic techniques is much like self-hypnosis. There is nothing mystical about the process. It is simply done, and the more we practice it the more proficient we become in achieving relaxation by self-effort.

Self-enhancement grows as we gain the upper hand through our own coping effectiveness. Once we develop the skill of relaxation, confidence builds an effective defense against self-doubt, and self-confidence is the nemesis of the neuroses!

For a demonstration of autogenic training, select a quiet setting (for now) and follow this script while sensing the physical effects.

Assume a comfortable posture in a chair with your legs uncrossed and feet resting on the floor, your arms at your sides or in your lap. (you can even follow this procedure at your seat in an airplane!)

Breathe in deeply; hold your breath for 2-3 seconds. Now, slowly exhale, relaxing deeper — and deeper.

Again, breathe in. Now close your eyes as you exhale, and sense the feeling of **heaviness** and **warmth.** Relax and sink heavily in the seat; note the gentle warming in your hands and feet as the circulation improves in your extremities.

Now, imagine and visualize a restful scene: a grassy knoll by a gentle stream, or a warm, soft, sunny beach with palm trees swaying... restful... warm... and relaxing.

Continue sensing the warmth and heaviness in your body while visualizing the restful setting.

Say the following words while focusing on your body:

- My arms and legs are heavy... I'm relaxed.
- My arms and legs are warm... I'm more relaxed.
- My heart beat is calm and regular.
    (Sense your pulse as it slows.)
- My breathing is relaxed and effortless.
    (Breathe slowly, regularly, not forced, relaxing as you exhale).
- I feel warmth in my abdomen... calm and relaxed.
- My forehead is relaxed... smooth and relaxed.
- My whole body is calm... relaxed... heavy and warm.

Now, repeat the sequence several times, sensing your entire body, relaxing any muscle tension while continuing to visualize the quiet, serene, and restful scene.

Repetition and practice will provide memorization of this procedure. You will find that it will be useful in airport waiting areas, or in your seat on board a plane. As you gain a positive control over your tense body states, you will note — a calm body, calms emotions as well.

Cognitive Thought Conditioning

As indicated earlier, our thoughts (cognitions) affect our bodies. Body control then becomes subject to conscious control, and, to an extent, many consider unconscious thought to have a similar influence on body function.

Cognitive relaxation techniques provide another method of calming the thoughts in a stressful setting. We can combat an anticipated catastrophe with a bit of reassuring self-talk, a cognitive process. It is possible to block compulsive thoughts that are intrusive and defy resistance by a competitive thought or diversionary action.

For example, when an irritating thought persists, visualize the letters STOP while saying the word to yourself in silence, then refocus your attention and concentrate on any unrelated task at hand or visualize a pleasurable activity.

In the seminars, snapping a rubber band placed around the wrist serves as an effective diverting action to escape from unwanted obsessive thoughts. When the sting is felt, the participants are instructed to shift their attention to a more pleasant thought or scene. It works! Many continue to wear the rubber band as a remembrance of its "stop-thought" effectiveness.

The unconscious mind cannot differentiate between the **real** and the **imagined**. Verbalized positive messages may provide a favorable influence on certain physical functions. These messages can become dominant thoughts in a relaxed state.

Cognitive inputs should be stated in the **first person** and **present tense**. As an example, follow this self-talk script:

- I'm in control of my body now... I'm relaxed.
- My body is quiet, my muscles relaxed... and resting.
- I can feel my body relaxed and healthy now.
- I can remain calm and under control in an airplane.
- I am more calm and my thoughts are directed to the pleasant time I will have when I fly... vacationing... visiting friends.
- I am now able to calm myself when I feel tense or anxious. I can control my body... my breathing... my heart rate... my muscles are smooth... and relaxed.
- I am looking forward to happy times with my friends and family... I am free when I fly!

By such conscious verbalizing of positive and pleasant thoughts, the mind-body influence becomes an effective means of reducing tension while enhancing the self-image.

Positive emotions mobilize the body's defenses to combat the stresses of fear and anxiety. Try to emphasize positive constructive thoughts, avoiding all doubt and negativeness. Replace chronic doubting with self-confidence. Such positive behavior can bring a welcome change for aerophobics!

Biofeedback: Voluntary Control of the Involuntary

For many, the term "biofeedback" suggests a mystical process; not so. It is a clear procedure and the effects on body functions are observable and convincing.

The principle of biofeedback allows us a measure of control over our involuntary autonomic nervous systems (ANS). In earlier times, control of the involuntary nerves was considered unlikely, and by many, impossible.

The central nervous system (CNS), which consists of the brain and spinal cord, permits voluntary activation of those body functions which it innervates (limbs and muscle system).

Automatically, the ANS controls such major functions as heart rate, blood pressure, digestion, and respiration without conscious effort by the person. We say the ANS controls those functions "involuntarily, because a person seemingly does not decide or "volunteer" to govern the various processes.

My early course work in physiology and anatomy seemed to make it clear that we had little if any control over our involuntary nerve functions, but that notion is no longer valid. Here's why.

Legitimate yoga practitioners dispelled this view with demonstrations of control in which they attained a state of near "suspended animation" with blood pressure or heart rate barely detectable by the most sophisticated instruments. Such control is undeniable evidence of the mind-body connection when mental activity (meditative or directed thought) is the vehicle used to effect measurable bodily changes.

Furthermore, it is now recognized that we have a greater potential to influence the physical condition by our thought processes than was ever before thought possible.

Body states of blood pressure, temperature, muscle tension , and brain-wave activity may be measured with relative ease. The term feedback describes the process of "feeding" measurement information back to the person providing the responses being measured.

In biofeedback training, the goal is to teach **awareness** and **self-control** of bodily conditions or functions and associate them with certain physical and emotional conditions. It is possible to alter or often relieve many physical states involving stress, tension, anxiety, hypertension (high blood pressure), headaches, and a variety of other discomforts.

By relaxing muscle tension, you can warm your body extremities (fingers and toes). This process occurs as a result of "freeing up" the circulation of warmed blood to the feet and hands. Noting this change, we may easily learn to increase the warming by further relaxation.

Normally, blood pressure will lower with the freer blood flow in accordance with the physical laws of hydraulics and thermodynamics. Behold, a supposedly involuntary system now responds to conscious control!

We can similarly measure muscle tension by electrical sensing devices (electromyography), and record changes in tension as we relax or become more tense, thus measuring direct evidence of our voluntary efforts. Of course, many body functions and muscles are already under conscious control, like the movements of arms and legs, quite unlike finger temperature and blood pressure. Granted, the temperature and blood pressure control is indirect, but fingers and toes still may be made to become warmer.

Picture this: fear produces tension; tension produces stress (or fatigue); stress, in turn, can increase fear — a classic vicious circle that can become an endless chain of misery. To break this circle, what better way is there to reduce the tension than by relaxing, which lowers the stress, and thus, reduces the fear? The circle is broken!

For those familiar with the Lamaze technique of painless childbirth, mothers similarly disrupt the "fear-tension-pain" cycle by tension reduction (using relaxation and breathing styles), which lessens the pain, in turn reducing the fear of pain.

Once they feel the letup in pain, they find that further relaxation brings wonderful relief, a grateful reward. Miraculous? Not really. Practice yields great benefits, as Lamaze mothers testify.

The payoff comes by using the technique when "under fire" **at delivery time.** The Lamaze principles are analogous to overcoming a fear of flying, provided the effort is made to counteract the fear **at flight time!**

The combination of autogenic training and biofeedback is highly compatible for inducing relaxation. Inexpensive temperature biofeedback units are available, complete with instructions for their use. Stress management programs include these techniques as an effective means of consciously reducing tension and stress. We can arrest the perverted grip of fear on our bodies by such autogenic relaxation and biofeedback conditioning.

The Role Of Medication: What Helps?

There is no evidence that medication alone will "cure" fear or phobias. In some cases, alcohol or Valium may bolster the person sufficiently to enable him to face up to an anxious or feared event. Such helps may be sufficient to alleviate discomfort on repeated situations, but dependency is a likely result that may further complicate living.

Intense emotions signal profound physical changes. Fear and anxiety have a potent effect on the feedback interaction between the mind and body.

Drugs are effective in the treatment of agoraphobia (mostly antidepressants), but recovery is unlikely without behavioral management and controlled exposure.

Psychologists opt for behavioral programs, and many are strongly resistant to reliance on medication, whereas psychiatrists usually favor medication first, although most concur with the need for behavior therapy in some form to augment the medical course in treating phobias. Other physicians may dispense anti-anxiety drugs on a trial-and-error basis, which often is sufficient. In any event, behavioral exposure is still necessary.

As an eclectic psychologist, I favor the prudent use of medication if it helps to initiate the encounter with flight, after one has learned the basics of stress/anxiety/fear management.

The combination of medication **and** behavior management forms an effective alliance for physicians and psychologists in combatting aerophobia. Participants in the aerophobia seminars are encouraged to consult their personal physicians for consideration of any appropriate medication.

The Role Of Attitudes

The greatest discovery of our generation is that a human being can alter his life by altering his attitudes.

William James

Our attitudes determine to a great extent our reactions to events in life. Dealing with stressful situations effectively requires an attitude of self-confidence in one's ability to cope with adversities.

The importance of positive mental attitudes is a central theme advanced by a popular genre of motivational lecturers such as Norman Vincent Peale, Paul Harvey, Denis Waitley, Zig Zieglar, W. Clement Stone, and Norman Cousins. Their personal successes have inspired many followers to develop attitudes of heightened self-confidence for overcoming stressful obstacles in their lives.

Psychologists consider attitudes are learned, much as our opinions and beliefs are acquired. Attitudes provide us with a potential readiness for reaction to all situations. And, of more importance, **our reactions to stress are often more disturbing than the stress itself!**

This view was advanced by the Roman philosopher, Epictetus, when he observed, ''Men are disturbed not by things, but by the views which they take of them.''

Could a change in views produce a change in attitudes? It's worthy of thought!

Research confirms even animals display attitude-like behaviors that influence their responses to stressful events.

For instance, a state of ''learned helplessness'' can be induced in laboratory animals (usually rats subjected to mild electric shock) that determines their reactions to a feared stimulus. Animals in control of termination of the shock fare much better than do their cohorts who are subjected to the same shock but are unable to control the undesirable stimulus. The ''helpless'' animals show significantly greater inappropriate behavior and physical change than those in control of the feared shock. Again, the reaction is intrinsically related to the severity of the consequence.

Humans have conquered dreaded illnesses by ''taking charge'' of their bodies through the use of extraordinary measures. The results, which have often baffled medical scientists, defy explanation.

A robust "will to live" in a patient is a welcome ally to physicians. In the best seller, *Anatomy of an Illness*, author Norman Cousins tells of his experiences and stresses the benefits of humor and mental attitude in curing your body.

For Cousins, even pain was seen to be affected and modifiable by one's attitude. He asks, "If negative emotions (attitudes) produce negative chemical changes in the body, wouldn't the positive emotions produce positive chemical changes?"

To answer this question, Cousins selected laughter and humor as his positive emotion to experiment with to lessen his discomfort from a painful, crippling, and degenerative arthritic-like disorder.

The results of Cousin's recovery propelled interest in his use of **humor** and **confidence** in not only dispelling his pain, but in alleviating his anxiety and depressive attitudes. The remission and curative effects of his illness still lack objective explanation, but Norman Cousins offers a challenge for scientists to account for his outcome with further research.

Again, we have evidence that in many instances, **it is not the event but our reactions to the event** that determine the outcome or consequences that befall us. Overreacting may indeed worsen a situation, as is certainly true with fear!

In a sense, can it be possible we cause our own effects? Why then, do we not **choose** to react in a manner that will benefit our efforts rather than add to our despair or fear? It is Cousins' view we are free to choose that course, with the proper attitude, which will yield a more favorable outcome. It's certainly conceivable and worthy of trial.

In overcoming fear, if attitude plays a major role in determining the outcome, why not choose positively? It worked for Norman Cousins (and untold others) in overcoming rational adversity which was more serious and life-threatening than **any** acquired irrational fear.

Attitudes do influence the outcome (success or failure) and this premise is central to gaining control over the irrational fear of flying. Victors in the seminars are living testimonies to the importance of their attitudes in gaining confidence in flying.

Those still persisting in their fears have yet to see the importance of choosing the proper attitudes of self-confidence and trust, which can push aside their doubts and the dread of air travel. Failing to make the choice, freedom from fear will continue to elude them, even though the choice is theirs to make.

FLIGHT PLANNING CHECK LIST

Use this check list as a guide in planning each trip on a commercial airline. Carry it with you and refer to it frequently during each flight. Do not rely on memory.

SMILE, BREATHE, and RELAX when SBR is on the check list.

PRE-FLIGHT:

Select a travel agent who will consider your individual needs for safety and convenience in travel plans.

1) Reservations: Plane, Hotel, ground transportation. Arrange early seat assignment.

2) Ticketing: Advance pickup is preferred.

3) Baggage plan: Proper wardrobe for climate and length of stay. Separate items for use in flight (Medication, extra glasses, reading, cards) from checked luggage.

4) Consider "practice run" to airport before actual departure date. Rehearse airport procedures.

AIRPORT PLAN:

Trip to airport: DO NOT RUSH! Allow extra time for traffic, car troubles, detours, parking. etc.

1) Ticket counter check-in for baggage and seat selection. Expect security screening. SBR

2) Boarding area. Consider use of rest rooms before boarding. Purchase late needs and reading materials. SBR during waiting time or delays — Read, browse shops, or visit with travel companion. AVOID FRUSTRATION!

BOARDING AIRCRAFT:

1) Locate seat, store carry-on items, coats etc. Adjust seat, air vents and seat belt (comfortably). SBR.

2) Announcements: Do not allow to excite! Passive attention is sufficient. Anticipate service — choices of beverage, meal selections, magazines etc.

3) Departure activities: distract self to cabin door closing and engine startup; visit with seat mate, read paper, listen to cassette music or relaxation tape. SBR!

IN-FLIGHT PROCEDURES:

1) TAKEOFF: Monitor time of takeoff run by counting. Limit attention to seat area only, disregard others. SBR!

2) ENROUTE: Enjoy service. Anticipate pleasantries of arrival — meeting friends, sightseeing etc. Use lavatory to refresh. Visit with seat mate, read, or rest.

3) TURBULENCE/WEATHER: SBR — Do not tense or brace body against bounces — it will soon become smooth! SBR!

4) DELAYS: EXPECT the UNEXPECTED with calmness! Attend to announcements as information — not alarms. Visit, read or rest. Easy does it — AVOID FRUSTRATION!

5) ARRIVAL/LANDING: Focus on meeting friends, baggage claim, transportation and events of the day. Landing delays are common. Praise yourself! YOU DID IT! A HAPPY LANDING!!

An audiocassette tape which is provided in the seminars is available for self-relaxation (autogenic training) for $6.50 post paid.

Order from:

WINGS PUBLICATIONS
P.O. Box 161
Mission, KS 66201

Chapter 8

EVERYTHING YOU'VE WANTED
TO KNOW ABOUT FLYING...
BUT WERE AFRAID TO ASK!

Failure is not daring to believe
Success is becoming a believer!

Denis Waitley, Seeds of Greatness

Should the wings flap up and down on a jetliner? What are all of the eery noises I hear in the cabin when I fly? When they shut the engines off right after takeoff, my heart stops dead still! **What if** all the engines should really stop? **What if** the pilot has a heart attack? **What if** we get hijacked?

All of these are fair questions and represent but a sampling of the questions that those in the seminars ask most frequently; endless "what-ifs" reflect the concerns of fearful flyers and their need for more technical information.

Explanations, even the simplest of answers, never alleviate all of the concerns underlying the questions. But, we do encourage questions. All of the doubts suggest an honest, concerned naivete in each inquiry. Before long, chuckles form the backdrop for each question, even those that are prefaced with "I know this sounds absurd, but, what if..." And so it goes.

Our ground rules assure there are no absurd questions, only uninformed or misinformed persons seeking honest, informed answers.

It helps to describe and discuss each issue, even to draw pictures of aerodynamic principles, or explain weather phenomena, especially turbulence and storms. Yes, even "wind shear and microbursts" are fair topics for discussion. We also review human factors of stress and fatigue along with current topics such as terrorism and hijackings.

The dialogue provides explanations, not excuses! **Explaining** serves to demystify and desensitize the issue. **Excuses** raise more doubt, adding to the chronic doubting that is already in abundance and only adds to a questioner's problems. **Confidence develops with belief and knowledge.**

Advancements and technologies in commercial air transport design in today's jet age are unparalleled in history. We consider the reliability and the safety of early-day transport airplanes, such as the Ford Tri-motor, to be spectacular in their era, but by today's standards, they were fraught with limitations.

When passenger flying began, comfort, weather flying capability, navigational aids, engine reliability, safety devices, ground support resources, and overall dependability were much sought-after goals, but they were not yet attained in those early days of air travel. Comfort was nil. Safety was marginal. Successful commercial flight was often limited to pitifully short distances.

By comparison, the DC-3 series in the 1930s revolutionized air travel with improved reliability. Still limited were comfort and a respectable range of non-stop travel. In 1936, the DC-3 range was thought remarkable just as we feel about today's transports. It soon became a reliable "workhorse" of modern air travel.

At the conclusion of World War II, the advent of four-engined, pressurized airliners, such as the Lockheed Constellations and DC-6 series, further revolutionized travel by air. The industry made major strides in added comfort and longer-range, non-stop flights. The multi-engine designs provided safe continuance of controlled flight even with a failed engine.

Technologies soon overwhelmed the industry. Amazing new principles in electronics, hydraulics, aircraft design, and engine power flourished. Safety improved remarkably. The air travelling public benefitted greatly from each advancement, and in short order, air passengers took for granted the unfolding of many "miracles" in air transportation.

The demand for larger planes that were capable of carrying heavier loads called for increased engine horsepower (thrust). Because of the limited reliability and power of piston engine designs, the jet engine, with its increased thrust, soon became the standard for commercial airliners.

By comparison, comfort in today's aircraft is without equal. Speeds have increased six-fold for the subsonic transports and tenfold in supersonic craft. The range of flight allows world-wide transoceanic crossings with ease.

The jet-powered transport heralded a new era for the air transport industry worldwide with major credit to be given to development of the jet engine. Added technological growth continues at an ever-expanding magnitude. Aerospace research, computer technology, metallurgy, and aerodynamic design continue to provide revolutionary change almost daily. True marvels in technology have made air transportation safer than ever in the history of aviation. Consider the following for example.

The Role of the Jet Engine

Let's review engine reliability by itself. Piston engines in the early 1930s performed remarkably if they achieved 100 hours of trouble-free operation, and they required complete overhaul, usually, after a few hundred hours of flying.

With irony, only marginal improvement was made over some 40 years of flying with piston engines. Major overhauls are in order on most of the late-model piston engines after each thousand hours of operation. In the interim, problems and corrective maintenance needs are a daily consideration.

This dramatic improvement in engine reliability when put into perspective, is part of my personal flying experiences during a 40-year career. As a command pilot, I welcomed the challenge to make the transition from pistons to turbojets. For many veteran pilots, jet training was more of a psychological experience than a technological awakening. The need for adaptive change was dramatic for many of us. We were "born-again flyers" by necessity when entering the jet age.

A review of my logbook covering the last twelve months of flying piston airplanes (1959-1960), revealed 13 engine faults or failures — each time disrupting scheduled flight operation! On at least four of those occasions, the fault was detected by fire-warning indications, which required the use of fire extinguishers to control the source of combustion.

Each engine problem required an unscheduled landing at an airfield short of the planned destination, creating a disruptive effect on the hoped-for reliability of our airline schedules. Such progress was questionable.

I might explain for the sophisticated traveller and experienced pilot, that most of the failures involved the turbo-compound piston engines. These engines were notorious for faults because of attempts to push piston engines for more thrust — far beyond reasonable limits. A minor maladjustment or component malfunction could lead to a precautionary shut-down, or ultimately, failure of the engine.

By comparison, with more than 21 years of flying turbojet airplanes (Convair 880, Boeing 707/720, Lockheed 1011, and the Jumbo Boeing 747), I had to shut-down fewer than 10 engines in flight! Alas, such progress was unfathomable!

Moreover, none of the jet engine problems disrupted what was otherwise normal flight operation from departure to destination. Remedial action was often taken merely as a precaution to limit any aggravated damage to the costly engine; had we needed it, the engine was still capable of providing thrust! We never compromised safety or schedule.

Two memorable occasions involving Boeing 707 transatlantic flights come to mind. Each one involved continuing more than two hours to destination on 3 engines — and still — the landing was made ahead of schedule! And, I may add, **never was the safety of the flight marginal!**

Whenever it was necessary to reduce power or to shut down a jet engine, the passengers were rarely aware we had taken such action. Unfortunately, passengers could tell immediately on piston airplanes because they could see the stopped propeller and would notice the change in the engine noise levels. Explanations were seldom sufficient to arrest the apprehension among the passengers, and often, the crew.

On jets there was little need for them to know when an engine developed a problem, since stopping a jet engine has little or no significant effect on flight performance.

For instance, on 4-engine jetliners there is little change in flight procedures with one engine shut down. On 3-engine planes the same holds reasonably true with one engine inoperative. In fact, when training on the L-1011 (a 3-engine jet) we learned a procedure for having "2 engines inoperative" When we asked the ground school instructor why the method was not called a "single engine" procedure (which in fact it was), he replied, unconvincingly, that it standardized terminology with **all** 2-engine inoperative practices — leaving an air of skepticism in the class, which was later dispelled.

All concern soon disappeared during the training in actual flight when we found to our satisfaction that on a "single engine," the Jumbo 1011 was capable of making an approach and landing... safely! It was a convincing performance by such a massive airplane.

Thrust, or horse power, in jets is rarely marginal, but the same was not true with the piston-powered airplanes. In fact, the reliable "old workhorse" DC-3 could not qualify for today's transport category certification because of its limited power (1100 to 1200 horsepower per engine) in the event of an engine failure on takeoff! It is still allowed to operate, but under a "grandfather clause" in the FAA regulations.

Piston engine failures, when they did occur, were not only more frequent but were much more critical to flight.

I am frequently asked the question, "What would happen if we lost all engine power (in today's jets) while at 35,000 feet?" There is stark amazement when I remark the airplane could "glide" for a distance of some 100 miles or more! (This distance is based on an average glide ratio of some fifteen miles for each mile of altitude, and 35,000 ft. equals approximately seven miles.) 100-miles of controlled, powerless flight is thought impossible, particularly by the chronic doubters, but when explained, it dispels a world of anxiety for the **believers!**

Many envision the plane would "come straight down and crashland!" That's grossly untrue, and further, the glide distance is sufficient to find a suitable airport or clear landing area in a majority of cases. (Over ten suitable airports lie in a 100-mile radius of Kansas City.)

Even after refuting the "crash-landing" misconception, I find many persist in their doubts and remain concerned about the capabilities of today's modern airliners. Again, doubt plagues them, and continues as one of their major problems.

The vast improvement in jet engine reliability has resulted in the FAA allowing overhaul time periods to be determined (by certain approved airlines) with no fixed limit on the accumulated number of hours in operation. The FAA's position reflects a mark of proved reliability in modern aircraft engines.

The design of the engines is such that all components are constantly monitored or recorded to register the slightest malfunction or wear. When a problem is detected, or a part exceeds tolerance, regulations require the maintenance crew to change the component immediately.

It is to the airline's advantage to make these corrections in a timely manner to avoid a more serious malfunction at a less opportune time, which results in considerably greater costs. Preventive maintenance is a benefit to both safety and economy and is a major guideline for the successful airlines today.

Benefits of Space Techonology

Advancement of other systems and components on jet airplanes has kept abreast of those gains made in the engine power plants.

Navigation systems for instance, are now fully self-contained — on board the aircraft — requiring no land radio navigational facilities for accurate computation to any destination on the surface of the Earth.

For example, the method of "inertial navigation," called INS, is the same principle as that used by astronauts on the space flights. This system will compute the course to any destination once it is programmed with the latitude and longitude of the desired position. The pilot engages the autopilot to the INS mode and proceeds to destination — with remarkable accuracy — nearly hands-off!

The INS system solves time and distance problems to a tenth of a nautical mile and a tenth of a minute. It also provides information about wind direction and velocity, groundspeed, wind-drift angle, and the time remaining to destination. Any part of this information is available to pilots at all times. (Unfortunately, it doesn't brew coffee.)

The INS accuracy is unquestionable, and a "redundancy" plan insures top reliability like that gained with multiple engines; there are three INS units for all transoceanic flights, and they cross-compare performances among all units continually. Any difference that develops in any one system, when compared to the other two units, requires investigation, providing a fail-safe condition for serving navigational needs and assured accuracy. In over eleven years use of INS navigation, I experienced only **five** malfunctions in a single INS unit. Never a problem!

The integrity of modern jet transports and their components undergoes continual scrutiny. FAA specialists in each field of technology mandate periodic maintenance inspections. Ongoing research by the manufacturers, the airlines, the government and academic researchers alike, assures the public that the industry maintains full awareness of the latest developments. Aerospace technologies are readily available for commercial use and each new development continues to benefit the air transport industry.

What About Air Traffic

The air traffic system causes a variety of concerns with the general public. Air traffic is a constant source of public and political debate. The air transport industry is subjected to unending criticism, for which there is little justification of the claims.

Again, opinions are more prevalent than facts in support of the negative allegations challenging the safety of air traffic control. In the writer's view, supported by data from the insurance industry, the air traffic control system as it exists in the United States today, **is acceptably safe** — and is the "model" for air traffic control — the World over!

But neither government nor industry will accept a status quo attitude in searching for safer means of managing the burgeoning volume of air traffic. Funds **are** available for the needed research and development, which will further improve the safe handling of air traffic.

Research in radar has received high priority to expand traffic and weather information gathering for both ground and airborne use. The "crowded skies" will become "decongested" as a result of this ongoing research. In the interim, the alertness of traffic controllers and flight crews alike is a constant priority for the safety of the air travelling public.

If at any time a professional pilot deems an unsafe traffic condition to exist, he must report the situation in full to the authorities. All such reports demand action and immediate correction.

The public has become aware of the term "near miss" in reporting cases in which two aircraft fly too close to each other. The term, near miss, is confusing and alarming, since if two objects nearly missed each other, it implies that they in fact hit each other! Such semantics are rather humorous, that is, if the consequences were not so severe.

Regarding the problem of air congestion, it is virtually impossible to accurately assess its severity. For example, during a recent month, the Chicago area reported four violations of "standard separation" between two airplanes, which stirred considerable public concern, including strong outcries from media sources. Further investigation revealed that the planes were no closer to each other than four miles at any time, and were **never** on a collision course — but this fact was apparently not as newsworthy!

Nevertheless, regulations required making the report because the required minimum separation for the situation was five miles when at the same altitude. True, the violations had occurred, but the incidents point to the conservative edge in safety that determines "safe distances" for the separation of aircraft.

Press coverage of aviation irregularities often falls short of telling the full story. Aviation accidents involve early reports by observers that are fraught with distortions which often result in erroneous speculation and reporting. Investigation is a lengthy and meticulous process.

Fears build when the media reporting overplays the incidents as near-gross tragedies when indeed they are not. Aerophobics are taunted by such reports, and they attend obsessively to each mention of an air disaster, adding to their dread of flying. Statistical facts and air safety data are seldom convincing, nor are they given equal time by the media. Unfortunately, each mishap serves only to confirm the doubts of the aerophobics and many in the travelling public as well.

Foreign nations including the more remote areas of newly emerging nations use U.S. air traffic control standards, and original training of their controllers occurs either in the U.S. or in the foreign nation itself with training by American consultants. As a result, English is the primary language for traffic control the world over. The International Civil Aviation Organization (ICAO) is the agency responsible for administering the regulation of air travel among the member nations worldwide.

Congestion of air traffic has been an ever-increasing problem with the growth of the air transport industry. It was a concern even in the DC-3 era of the 1930s, but as traffic expands, computer technologies, radar, and navigational aids are continually improving to meet the increasing demands on air space.

The establishment of stringent criteria for fail-safe air traffic control is a primary goal of the aviation industry worldwide. Great progress occurring today in technologies will further enhance the safety and reliability of air travel.

Data in Chapter One support the view that air travel is remarkably safe. The industry never rests in its search for higher standards of safe air travel. Dispelling doubt while assuring a fearful passenger of a safe journey is not an easy task, but learning more of the technical factors seems to relieve some of the apprehension for those willing to believe rationally. Too often, emotion blocks belief, a condition that psychologists know well, but for which they have yet to find the solution.

As Denis Waitley stated, "Success is becoming a believer." Hence, overcoming an irrational fear demands one overcomes his disbelief. The trick is to become a believer — and success will follow.

What About the Weather?

It is difficult to conceive of any mode of travel that is not affected by weather, and the airplane would appear to be more vulnerable than other vehicles. Not so, and furthermore, aviation has made greater progress in coping with weather problems than any other mode of transportation. Still, the elements of nature, on occasion, do inflict their disruptive influences on air travel.

Intense weather movements plague surface travel more severely than they do air travel, and the effects last longer. For example, floods, tornadoes, and snowstorms obviously imperil travel at the time of occurrence, but the after-effects continue to interfere with surface vehicles for extended periods. The airplane is often able to resume travel sooner, or, if in flight, to circumvent many storms with little interruption to service. Countless times the airlines have routinely operated "over the weather" unaffected by weather conditions on the Earth's surface far below.

In four decades, aviation has advanced sufficiently in all-weather flying that visibility restrictions hold little problem in completing schedules. "Blind flying" became a reality as early as 1929 when Jimmy Doolittle made the first takeoff and landing solely "by instruments."

Today's jet transports perform this feat routinely with "zero ceilings" and visibilities that would have ground travel slowed to a snail's pace. And instrument landings can be performed safely and accurately by the automatic pilot, while the human pilots merely monitor the performance. Aviation, by no means controls the weather, but advancements in radar, communications, and aircraft performance have tamed those conditions that held severe threats to early flight (fog, ice, snow, and severe windstorms).

It is rare indeed, for in-flight icing conditions to be a problem as they often were with propeller-driven aircraft. Jet aircraft fly at altitudes that provide escape from the majority of weather hindrances early pre-jet transports were forced to endure.

TURBULENCE is the one major concern mentioned most frequently by aerophobics. The slightest bounces seem to bring on intense fear and discomfort. They have a dread of thunderstorms with lightning, and a fear of sharp jolts whenever the plane bounces or pitches about.

Pilots dislike rough air more for the invasion of their passengers' comfort than for any fear of structural damage to the plane. Pilots take great effort to avoid turbulence at all times, but when it is unavoidable, safe speed limits are targeted, and they seek changes in altitude or the flight course that will give their passengers a smoother ride.

Still, even an "innocent air bounce" results in a muscle tension, "poker stiff" reaction by most air travellers, which only intensifies the shock to the body. A relaxed posture serves to soften the jolts of air turbulence. DO NOT "BRACE" YOUR BODY against rough air!

Here is an exercise we offer in the seminars to ease the fear of turbulence:

1) Stand erect with your legs stiff and knees locked.

2) Abruptly, unlock your knees and drop toward the floor, but catch yourself sharply, with a jolt.

3) Visualize and sense the effects on your body, the abdomen particularly, as you repeat the exercise several times.

This maneuver is a reasonable simulation of the effects of "light turbulence" that is the type we encounter most frequently. A much sharper "drop and stop" maneuver may approximate what pilots refer to as "moderate turbulence," which we encounter less often. This exercise is valuable to get the feel of the bodily forces that when visualized in flight, will lessen the fear and discomfort of being jolted about in rough air.

To further diminish the fear of turbulence, it helps to visualize (and say to yourself) the airplane is "only on a bumpy, country road — for a brief spell." Turbulence seldom lasts, and by guided imagination, it will be little more than a tolerated nuisance to the passenger, as it is to the flight crews.

"Severe turbulence" is a rarity in flight, and when such extreme conditions are likely, the FAA broadly circulates warning notices to all aircraft in the affected area. In four decades of flying, I encountered severe turbulence fewer than a half dozen times — and never did we have any loss of control or structural damage to the plane!

"Wind shear," associated with landing mishaps in recent years, is capable of reaching severe levels of intensity. Steps have been taken to improve the detection of potential wind shear in airport vicinities. Doppler radar sites are being installed at major airports to provide further warning to the flight crews of impending surface wind-shifts.

Cockpit instrumentation (including the INS), helps to warn the pilots of abrupt changes in wind direction and velocities. The FAA and airlines have developed crew training and landing approach procedures that provide added safe margins for those rare occasions when wind shear is a possibility.

Turbulence while at cruising altitudes, is usually associated with the jet streams that traverse the airways at the higher altitudes. Often, it is unannounced and does little more than rattle items in the galleys or flip loose items about the cabin. We recommend passengers wear their seat belts "comfortably" fastened throughout the flight. That simple precaution can dampen surprise bounces adequately with little more than a beverage spill, and the body-jostling will rarely exceed the knee-drop exercise.

Recent acts of highjacking, worldwide, have given a "legitimacy" for avoiding flight by many air travellers, including those who normally enjoy flying. Unfortunately, each event is given excessive exposure by the media, which only adds to the fear of those who already dread flying.

Intelligence task forces have researched the terrorism problem with endless reams of reports on the topic. The problem is addressed in the seminars with candid honesty — in a 4-point plan — for coping with such an unlikely event as being highjacked. The assumption is made that a victim's options are pitifully few, hence, coping is best accomplished by the following:

1) CONTAIN the problem. Remain calm and avoid escalation.
2) COMPLY with the captors and the crew. Avoid heroics.
3) CONSERVE energy. Rest and avoid fatigue.
4) BUY TIME. Be creative and avoid showdowns.

The rationale for this concise plan is thought to provide a guide line for coping with an otherwise intolerable situation, even though it has been calculated the risk of being highjacked today is no greater than the chances of being "struck by lightning!" Also, having a plan serves to make one feel less like a victim.

It is difficult to exhaust the supply of questions aerophobics pose during the hangar flying sessions in the seminars. Nonetheless, we make every effort to meet each concern head-on, whether logical or absurd, and participants do feel relief when we explain some of the mysteries of flight. Although aviation today approaches the miraculous at times, few mysteries remain; only a lack of knowledge by some of the public. Being informed helps.

Jumbo Jet Trivia of Note

Just imagine: the Wright Brothers' first historic flight covered a distance shorter than the 225 foot length of a Boeing Jumbo 747! The top of the tail of the 747 is over six stories high (63 feet). The total wing area is greater than a university basketball court (5500 square feet). And, on and on it goes — astounding facts that few persons are aware of as they take air travel for granted today.

Comfort in flight is proportional to the size of the aircraft. The larger the craft, the smoother the ride! A good analogy would be to compare a rowboat to the Queen Mary for crossing the Atlantic Ocean!!

In fact, for "first flyers," a flight on a jet airliner can be a dramatic let-down if they are expecting a sensation of speed or height. The cabins of smaller narrow-body jets (DC-9s, Boeing 727/737s) resemble a small theater; wide body jets (Boeing 747/767, Lockheed L1011, DC-10) are reminiscent of a large hotel lobby or a wide-screen movie theatre. The feeling of flying is non-existent, which is the most impressive reaction noted by those experiencing their first flight.

Technically, the jumbo 747 has an amazing array of data that are interesting for trivial consideration:

1) Gross weight is over 750,000 pounds on most models, of which, 500 pounds of paint are used for average markings.

2) A spiral staircase in the forward section allows access to the cockpit and upper lounge area (for 20 to 60 passengers), lavatory, and serving bar. (A plan exists to extend the upper deck the full length of the fuselage and accommodating up to 800 passengers!)

3) Fuel capacity of 47,000 gallons (316,000 pounds!) is enough to keep a family car running for 60 years.

4) The parts catalog is 3 feet high containing 12,000 pages listing most of the four-and-one-half million parts.

5) One 747 engine develops more power, or thrust, (50,000 pounds) than all three engines combined on a 727.

6) The eight-foot diameter opening of a 747 engine is equal to the average room ceiling height.

7) There are well over 100 miles of wiring in a 747.

8) A fully provisioned 747 has 491 coffee cups, 972 plates, 847 glasses, 176 bottles of wine (6 oz.), and 25 gallons of liquor/liqueurs. (Well-stocked for many "happy hours" aloft.)

9) The cost of a new DC-3 in 1940 was approximately $25,000, which is insufficient to pay for one fuel fill-up of a 747 today! Incredible?

My airline flying career which spanned four decades, from the DC-3 to 747, continues to impress me with the miraculous growth of commercial aviation.

Few air travellers can appreciate fully the scope of technical advancement achieved, accompanied by the increased comfort, reliability, and above all, safety in performance. Those who remain fearful of flying must rid themselves of their attitudes of skepticism, pessimism, and negativism that persist in limiting their confidence in flight.

Flying is no longer miraculous. Rather, it is the culmination of scientific progress conducted by dedicated individuals who are "believers" in their chosen careers.

Become a believer, and become free from the fear that confines... the world awaits those who dare to believe!

Chapter 9

YOU ARE IN GOOD HANDS

*Persistent Training is the Key to TWA Excellence and
the Foundation of Public Trust in All of Us*
Jack Frye, President, TWA

The above inscription appears in the lobby of the TWA Jack Frye Training Center in Kansas City, Missouri. It typifies the importance of public trust and the need for high standards of performance by employees throughout the air transport industry.

Jack Frye, a pioneer leader in airline history, held a deep sense of need for safety and excellence as uppermost for the ultimate success of commercial air travel. He lived a "credo of concern" for a safe and reliable transition from surface to air transportation. Jack Frye had his own brand of "passion for excellence."

Even before assuming the leadership of TWA in 1934, Jack Frye held forth great pride for the professionalism of piloting. Among his pilots, he was acclaimed a "pilot's pilot," which is the highest form of peer praise for a fellow airman.

A major highlight of my airline flying career came about when I served as Jack Frye's co-pilot. And, a co-pilot is often the best judge of his Captain's abilities and personal attributes. Aviation benefitted greatly by the leadership of men with Jack Frye's vision and dedication to progress and safety in air transportation.

As President of TWA, Jack Frye was personally close to his coworkers. In the formative years of the airline, his frequent personal contact with the TWA family of employees succeeded in building an esprit de corps that was unequalled in industry. He personified the principle of "management by walking around" that marks the successful manager of today. Public trust was a treasured goal of Jack Frye, and achieving public confidence was his greatest triumph in a career unmatched in early airline leadership.

Skeptics became believers in air travel once they came to know the Jack Fryes, Eddie Rickenbackers, C. R. Smiths (American Airlines), Bill Pattersons (United Airlines), and Bob Six (Continental Airlines) all of whom were leaders of early-day airlines with such vision and dedication to safe air service.

If I were to choose any career again, it would be once more as an airline pilot. I could not have had a more interesting, challenging, and rewarding profession.

Regardless, desire to be an airline employee is not enough. Most airlines have a rigorous selection process of applicants for each job classification. It is not unusual to select 100 employees from a thousand or more applicants for flight crew positions.

College degrees are required by the major airlines for flight crew openings, and are given preference for the majority of ground personnel applicants. Technical skills must be confirmed by FAA licenses in the case of pilots and mechanics. References and personal background data must confirm applicants are stable, unblemished in character, and skilled in their chosen work.

Public trust is essential for the success of any company, especially so for airlines. Employee pride runs deep throughout any successful airline. The corporate images represented by logos, color schemes and traditions are strongly indoctrinated in new employees by the "old-timers." Company pride and allegiance continue to grow throughout employees' careers regardless of their task assignment.

SAFETY is the hallmark of the transportation industry. Airline employees feel the tragedy of each accident, and their concern is no less even when a mishap occurs on a competing carrier. Concern is the very fabric of the industry.

Admittedly, progress in the air transport industry has suffered on occasion by tragic occurrences. Nevertheless, the advancement from the Ford Trimotor of the '20s to the Jumbo 747 of the '70s must be regarded as a remarkable quantum leap forward in aircraft design and safety.

An assessment of my career from the DC-3 to the 747 brings to mind even minor incidents caused my colleagues and me to remain ever more alert to safety. The authorities conduct meticulous investigations of air mishaps in order to correct the causes as an obvious safeguard against any recurrence.

Major mishaps are of global concern to all facets of the industry. Governments, corporations, and manufacturers constantly center their efforts on achieving the safest practices possible. Advancements in air safety are a continuing by-product of these efforts. There is some positive compensation in knowing tragedy is not always in vain; some good always results.

Meet Your Cockpit Crews

Cockpit crew members (pilots and engineers) maintain a low profile by and large, despite Hollywood's best efforts and the likes of John Wayne, Charlton Heston, Gregory Peck, or George Kennedy. The creed of the Air Line Pilots Association (ALPA), SCHEDULE WITH SAFETY, has stood firmly for more than fifty years of its existence.

Airline pilots regard themselves as highly-skilled professionals, which they are. They never rest on once-acquired skills. Proficiency maintenance is a way of life. Training is ongoing; recurrent training and flight checks are routine throughout a pilot's career.

Overall, pilots must demonstrate competency in three areas:

1) Knowledge — obtaining necessary and sufficient information to meet rigid standards of performance.

2) Skill — acquiring abilities to perform the variety of tasks, competently and reliably.

3) Experience — functioning successfully over a long period while maintaining high standards in an exemplary manner.

Few, if any, among other kinds of professionals are subject to such stringent performance surveillance throughout their careers.

Additionally, pilots must demonstrate competency in actual flying trip observations by FAA and company supervisory pilots. The FAA conducts instrument flight checks twice a year on training hops and in modern simulators to assure that pilots maintain high standards of performance. Recurrent ground school and emergency training is an annual requirement.

What other profession can you think of that is subjected to inspection by a governing agent during the routine performance of their duties at any time, without notice? Federal Air Carrier inspectors (FAA) will observe actual flight operations from the cockpit at any time they may choose. These ''spot checks'' are in addition to the periodic six-month and annual training proficiency flight checks.

Ground schooling and flight training are mandatory each time a pilot becomes qualified on a different airplane. A pilot must study some three months in ground school, simulator training and line instruction before assignment to his new crew position.

Again, the FAA inspectors monitor the progress throughout this training. This system of checks and balances has each crew member under constant scrutiny.

Like continued training, regular physical examinations are an accepted routine for airline crew members. Captains must submit to FAA physicals every six months with an EKG annually. Any illness must undergo a complete review before renewal of the pilot's medical certification.

Copilots and engineers must take FAA physical exams annually; that's why most major airlines have aeromedical staffs for monitoring the health of their flight crews. These airlines require yearly company physicals in addition to the periodic FAA examinations.

Major airlines are quite liberal in granting sick leave with pay, discouraging any monetary incentive to try to fly when an individual is even mildly indisposed by illness.

An *Evaluative Survey of Disabilities Among Airline Pilots* was the subject of my Master's thesis in 1960. Data gathered at that time yielded conclusive evidence to confirm **airline pilots are considerably healthier** than the general population. This was a tribute to:

1) Rigid physical standards for original selection of pilots,

2) Preventive health maintenance examinations. It's another plus for prevention, in man as well as machine!

In-flight incapacitation of a flight crew member is a rarity indeed, with the exception of the dramatics found in B movies and TV specials. For the "chronic doubters," cockpit crew members are trained in all cockpit duties and are competent to perform other duties in the absence of any one crew member.

Furthermore, state-of-the art technologies in aircraft and systems design make it possible for one pilot crew member to operate and land solo — even in a jumbo jet!

Let's review some composite data on pilots presently employed on a major U.S. airline, namely, TWA. Captain Vern Laursen, Vice President of Flight Training for TWA, provided this recent capsule look at TWA's pilot ranks:

1) Mean age of Captains is 51 years and an average of 25 years of TWA flying seniority and experience. Additionally, all of these pilots have had considerable flight training prior to joining TWA.

2) Average of 15 thousand hours of flying time. This figure translates into some six thousand takeoffs and landings per pilot.

3) More than 18 years of copilot or engineer experience before becoming Captain. In the 1940s, copilots rarely flew more than a year or two before being "upgraded" to Captain.

4) All have some college and/or military training with a majority holding college degrees, now a basic requirement for all new pilot applicants.

5) A variety of flying experiences gained in domestic and international flying worldwide, encountering the vagaries of weather, government regulations, foreign affairs and political upheavals, all the while adhering to the professional ethics and standards of the Air Line Pilots Association.

TWA's flight crews are typical of many of the other major long-standing U. S. airlines. Similarly high credentials may not be reflected among those airlines that have emerged since government deregulation of the airline industry in 1978. Such flight crew experience, unfortunately, is less likely among the "new generation" airlines.

An intriguing profile of pilots appeared in the *U. S. Naval Flight Surgeon's Manual* in 1968. This view of pilot experience is particularly interesting in describing the "maturational processes" of a pilot's career. These levels of maturity may aptly describe any pilot, whether airline, military or civilian. The four stages of pilot maturation were depicted as follows:

THE GLAMOROUS YEARS — In the first years of flying there are few inhibitions resulting from age or experience. Much personal satisfaction derives from the mastery of a powerful and potentially dangerous instrument. Observations strongly suggest the personalities of successful (military) aviators, are characterized by a great "mastery drive." They fly dangerous aircraft in a dangerous manner because the aircraft and the missions are there.

INCREASING CAUTION — In the next few years, the pilot has become aware of his limitations and those of his aircraft. He has had narrow escapes, may have had an accident himself, and has lost friends who were admittedly as competent as he.

CONTROLLED FEAR OF FLYING — There then follows a period of increasing conservatism balancing any tendency toward recklessness which may have existed at the earlier periods. The pilot is at the peak of perfection. He knows he can be killed, tries to avoid it, and takes great pride in being a true professional. The developing caution of this period may be considered preparation for the aging of the pilot's physical and physiological capabilities.

THE SAFE YEARS — From this point on, the pilot's great experience, combined with the conservatism of his years, make his flying the safest of his career!

This last stage of maturation best describes the level of maturity and expertise attained by the cockpit crews on the major airlines today. Considering the maturity and experience prevalent among the flight crews of the major scheduled airlines, you may be assured that YOU ARE IN GOOD HANDS!

Crew Coordination: Exercise in Excellence

Pride in professionalism sustains a cockpit crew member to a dedication of excellence in his daily job performance. The same dedication holds true for other members of the airline team of employees. There is a common bond between flight and ground crews that is given less recognition by the public in the day-to-day routine of airline operation.

Public acclaim of ground support employees is often lacking. Even flight crews are guilty, at times, of taking for granted the contribution and valuable resource support of the ground crews and dedicated non-flying professionals. The fact is, crew coordination between flight crew members and ground crews is the essence of safe operation.

For example, flight attendants are often glamorized with lesser recognition of the safety contributions they provide while serving their passengers. Mention of Flight Attendant Uli Dericksen (in Chapter 2) is a recent example of professional concern for the safety and well-being of those assigned to her care. Aviation history continues to repeat itself with such tales, bordering on the heroic.

For instance, Nellie Granger, an early-day TWA Hostess of the 1930s, became a legend as she aided survivors of a crash. She trudged down a mountainous slope in a mid-winter storm to seek rescuers. Airline history is replete with Nellie Grangers and Uli Dericksens, none of whom will ever be forgotten by their peers.

Present day training of flight attendants stresses the importance of safety and survival training. Service and passenger comfort remain secondary to safety factors throughout a flight attendants career. In-flight service is a delightful experience (even for apprehensive passengers) when cockpit and cabin crews coordinate their efforts to achieve a safe and comfortable level of flight operation.